Praise for this book:

"If you're thinking about retirement, you must read **When I Retire**. This easy-to-read, easy-to-use book will not only inspire you to make your retirement the best it can be, but it gives you practical tools and guidance that empower you to actually make it happen."

> —Steve Vernon, FSA, author, **Money For Life** and **Recession-Proof Your Retirement Years.**
> www.RestOfLife.com

"Everything you need to think about regarding retirement but didn't know who to ask. I love this book, and recommend it highly if you are (1) thinking about retiring, (2) making plans to retire, or (3) thinking about making plans to retire. The tone of the book is optimistic, encouraging, and non-threatening, without being pie-in-the-sky about retirement. It's a reliable and encouraging companion on the sometimes-stressful road to anticipating your retirement. Don't leave (or stay) home without it!"

> —Ed Jacobson, PhD, MBA, author, **Appreciative Moments: Stories and Practices for Living and Working Appreciatively.** www.EdwardJacobson.com

"Andy Landis has given us the check-lists for the rest of our lives! In a series of bite-sized chapters he offers a series of considerations, lists, resources and quotes from the experts: those who have already retired. They cover every aspect of a life set loose from the constraints, joys and concerns of work. Take a chapter at a time—in your own time—and begin to engage yourself in this next, and maybe even best, part of your life."

> —Dan Kennedy, Career and Life Coach
> www.ResultsThatMatter.com

"Leonardo DaVinci said, 'Simplicity is the ultimate sophistication.' Andy has the gift of simplifying the very complex in his retirement insights, thereby delivering practical and actionable wisdom. This book is a must-read for anyone near, at, or in retirement."

> —John Busacker, President, INVENTURE—the Purpose Company, and Founder, Life-Worth, LLC

"*When I Retire* is a delightful read. Filled with great quotes from retirees' own observations, you'll want to go through it numerous times. It provides excellent lists of things to do and think about, broken down into key categories. Landis nicely adds his own wisdom, covered in 18 short chapters packed with insight, humor, and dreams of adventure."
—*Tom Washington, author,* **Interview Power**
www.cmr-mvp.com

"At a time when so much is up in the air and filled with uncertainty, Andy Landis's advice contained in **When I Retire** offers solid and practical help. His common-sense recommendations walk you through a confusing maze of retirement planning information and engage you in identifying and executing solutions that work for you. This should be on everyone's nightstand who is contemplating how to make ends meet in a world that fights against that end."
—*Lee White, Former Regional Vice-President of AARP*

"This is a must-read for baby boomers and those just embarking on a career and preoccupied with the demands of entering the workforce. Never has retirement planning been more crucial to your financial survival in later life. There is no judgment here from Andy Landis; just basic no-nonsense guidance about what to do now! You sense his passion about helping folks steer clear of landmines along the road to retirement. Give this to someone you love."
—*Bob McCormick, Money101 Host on CBS radio in Los Angeles*

"This book packs so much good information into one place it's like free time in the candy store! I've always wondered when Andy would take all the great knowledge packed in his brain and the fantastic (and sometimes tragic) stories of retirement that he's heard and put them both together in a way that helps individuals and couples plan their sunset years. I wonder no more—here it is!"
—*Steven "Shags" Shagrin, JD, CMC®, CFP®, CRPC®, CRC®, RLP®, www.PlanningForLife.info*

Also by Andy Landis:
Social Security: The Inside Story

"Best explanation of Social Security I've ever seen in print. I'm a retired Social Security Claims Representative and I rate this book as the best explanation of Social Security benefits I've ever seen. The writer's style is great and he has a nice, friendly approach. It's not an easy subject, but he explains things in a simple, understandable fashion." (★ ★ ★ ★ ★ —top rating)
>—*Amazon.com reader*

"I've found Andy's book to be absolutely essential for anybody planning their retirement. Andy tells you how to get the most from Social Security, which can add many thousands of dollars to your lifetime payouts. And his info on Medicare helps you navigate the complex rules, so that you minimize your out-of-pocket medical expenses." (★ ★ ★ ★ ★ —top rating)
>—*Steve Vernon, FSA, President, Rest-of-Life Communications and author of **Money For Life** and **Recession-Proof Your Retirement Years***

"This should be mandatory reading for rookie as well as veteran financial planners. The author lays out the often confusing "world" of Social Security in an understandable and entertaining fashion. The book's title says it all." (★ ★ ★ ★ ★ —top rating)
>—*David Koch, CFP®*

"Fantastic resource on all things Social Security!!! This is a great book that covers everything you need to know about Social Security. As a Certified Financial Planner®, I have referenced this book numerous times to help plan with my clients. The book is written in easy to understand language and covers pretty much anything you need to know. He uses great examples and provides many links to additional resources. This is a must-have for anyone in the financial services industry or anyone who wants to truly maximize and understand their benefits." (★ ★ ★ ★ ★ —top rating)
>—*Tom Faley, CFP®*

"Excellent. Easy to read. Much helpful information. Mr. Landis has succeeded in making a very complicated subject comprehensible to the average reader. All my questions about how the system works were answered. I appreciated the fact that Mr. Landis was employed by the Social Security Administration for many years and was able to give an insider's account of procedures and benefits. Many thanks for this very helpful book! (★ ★ ★ ★ — Amazon.com rating)"

> *--Amazon.com reader*

"A Perfect 'Layman's' Guide To Social Security. This book provides a very thorough, yet practical explanation of Social Security in an easy to read format. This is a great guide for almost anyone wanting a better understanding of not only how the program works, but how it will work for them as an individual participant." (★ ★ ★ ★ ★ —top rating)

> *--Matthew P. Jarvis, Chartered Financial Consultant*

"Landis does for Social Security what J.K. Lasser and others have done for taxes—provide reliable, understandable, and comprehensive guidance."

> *--Booklist*

"In a market full of manuals on Social Security and Medicare, this new book is the first that provides a comprehensive review of the regulations and at the same time explains how the Social Security Administration works."

> *--Jon Robert Steinberg, **New Choices for Retirement Living***

"For anyone who is approaching eligibility, [this book] is a very useful resource. Recommended."

> *--Midwest Book Review*

"Your book will, no doubt, help numerous individuals as they plan for their future. **The Inside Story** is not only full of important information, but also easy to read. You have made a complex subject understandable."

> *--Horace Deets, former Executive Director, AARP*

"An excellent, readable book on the complex story of Social Security. Every family should have one."

--*Elwood N. Chapman, author of* **Comfort Zones: A Practical Guide for Retirement Planning**

"This is by far the most useful book on Social Security that I have seen. I am particularly enthused by the organization that helps to find answers to specific questions and by the examples that are used for explanations. A job well done!"

--*Eugene O. Lieberg, Coordinator Retirement Planning Seminars, Boeing Defense and Space*

"Andy Landis makes the complexities of Social Security easy to understand. This well-organized book covers all of the important Social Security topics. The question and answer section and the numerous real-life examples are especially helpful. I highly recommend this expertly guided tour of Social Security."

--*Ray Eads, President, Wealth Management Northwest*

When I Retire

The Fastest, Easiest Way
To Make Your Retirement
Fun, Fulfilling, and Significant

Andy Landis
THINKING RETIREMENT
www.andylandis.biz

Have fun designing
your retirement !

Andy Landis

When I Retire:
The Fastest, Easiest Way To Make Your Retirement
Fun, Fulfilling, and Significant

By Andy Landis
THINKING RETIREMENT
www.andylandis.biz

2012.1

Library of Congress Cataloging-in-Publication Data

Landis, Andrew S.
When I Retire: The Fastest, Easiest Way To Make Your Retirement Fun, Fulfilling, and Significant
by Andy Landis.
$14.95 Softcover

ISBN-10: 1469904802
ISBN-13: 978-1469904801

Library of Congress Cataloging Number (LCCN): 2012912951
1. Retirement—Planning. 2. Retirement—Psychological aspects.
I. Landis, Andy   II. Title
HQ 1062.L   646.790973

This book is dedicated to you, the reader,
and the "new you" that will emerge in your retirement

And to Kay
I can't wait to share post-work life with you

CONTENTS

ACKNOWLEDGEMENTS

Many, many thanks to the hundreds of retirees who have answered my simple question: "How's it going?" Your experiences, challenges, spirit, and wisdom are my chief inspiration.

Thanks to the tens of thousands of retirees and pre-retirees I've met over the past 35 years through my work at Social Security, AARP, Ida Culver House Ravenna, Senior Services, Weyerhaeuser, and especially in my own practice, Thinking Retirement. You have shared so much and opened my mind and heart.

I am inspired by the work of John Nelson, Carol Anderson, Richard Johnson, Mitch Anthony, William Bridges, Rein Selles, Doug Shadel, Karen Kent, George Kinder, Bob Veres, and many more, too numerous to name. Thank you for providing an intellectual framework.

I am enormously grateful for the care and attention of colleagues who read early drafts of this book and offered their expert suggestions. Steve Vernon, Ed Jacobson, Dan Kennedy, John Busacker, Tom Washington, Lee White, Bob McCormick, "Shags" Shagrin, and Jo Landis, you guys are just too much. Thank you.

Special thanks to the pioneers and mentors, Pat Goelzer, Eugene Lieberg, and Helen Dennis, who blazed the trail. It is an honor to walk behind you.

A note on the "In Their Words" retiree quotations throughout the book: These are actual accounts from real retirees. In many cases they are exact quotes (or as exact as I could recall at my next opportunity to jot them down). In some cases they are paraphrased. For example, the passage in the "Spouse/Partner" chapter about the house in two wings is part of a much longer story involving the building of the house and the discovery that more psychological "space" was needed than they imagined. Most of the passage is a near-quote to capture the essence. The punch line is a direct quote.

INTRODUCTION

Get out your pencil. This is a book you will mark up.

The purpose of this book is simple: to inspire you to plan and live an *abundant* retirement, in the fastest, easiest way possible.

An abundant retirement has nothing to do with money. You don't have to be in the top tax bracket or have millions in savings to have abundance. An abundant retirement is a retirement that's worth living—that makes you eager to get up every day, with things to do, people to see, and something to look forward to.

Let's move your thinking beyond surviving to *thriving.* Let's banish dreary aimlessness and empty hours from our retirement thinking. Let's build a life of engaging and fulfilling activities, healthy relationships, discovery, and personal growth. You might even aim for retirement *significance,* a life that has a positive and lasting impact on those around you.

That's summed up in this book's subtitle, "**Fun, Fulfilling, and Significant.**"

This book will *not* tell you:

- How much money you need to retire
- How to invest your retirement funds
- Why you can never afford to retire
- How Boomers will change all the "rules" about retirement
- What to do when you retire

Instead, it puts forward hundreds of inspirations—ideas, quotations, real retirees' stories, goal-setting exercises, and resources—to help you make retirement the best time of your life. The entries aren't meant to be all-inclusive (by any means!), but offer ideas that will jump-start your own thinking. Add a dash of your own imagination and stir until you can hardly wait to live your retirement dreams.

The main differences between retirement and work life are: Less money (probably), much more time, and much more autonomy (freedom). In short, you'll have more of your life that *you* are in charge of.

It's your choice: you can fritter away your new-found time with empty hours, TV, and busy-work. Or you can see it as the opportunity of a lifetime. An opportunity to live better than you ever have, doing what you want to do, when you want, with whomever you want. That's right: Your life is finally *yours*. You can do what you always wanted to do. You can be who you always wanted to be.

In fact, you can do what you were always *meant* to do, and be who you were always *meant* to be.

Don't get me wrong. You can have all the "down-time" you want, for just hanging out—what the kids call "chillin'." But if that's *all* you did, you might find yourself going downhill. You'd be bored, and pretty soon you'd be lonely, too, because you'd be so bor*ing* people would drop you.

So as you look ahead to your retirement—or think about the rest of your existing retirement—aim a little higher. You've worked all your life for this time, the time that is truly yours. Make it worthwhile. Make it a life that will be the envy of your workmates and earn the respect of your partner and friends.

This book is meant to ignite your thinking about your retirement. It's not meant to be the final word—far from it. If it moves you to write down at least one idea that you want to pursue in retirement, it's accomplished its mission.

But there's a lot more here than that.

Working with thousands of retirees and pre-retirees for the past 35 years, I've heard a lot of different stories, including some retirement disasters. (Remember, retirement isn't for everyone, and I certainly hope it's not forced on you.) Of all the stories, a common refrain comes from some 95% of retirees, something like, "This is the best time of my life! You should do it as soon as you can!" I hope this **compact book** helps you make your retirement the very best time in your life.

Using this book is incredibly simple:

- Peruse the lists of activities and attitudes, the quotations, and the retiree stories, in any order.
- Checkmark the ones that interest you.
- Fill in the blank lines with ideas of your own. Scribble in the margins if necessary. Maybe start a three-ring binder, scrapbook, or computer file to hold all your ideas—especially if this is an e-book, or loaned to you!
- Build your personal retirement plan using your best ideas, in simple "ABC" steps.
- Finally, get out there and have the time of your life.

I would never presume to tell you how to live in retirement, but I hope I can help you discover your own best life.

Dwight Eisenhower said, "Plans are useless but planning is indispensable." May the planning you do here become an indispensable tool in building your abundant retirement.

CHAPTER ONE

RE-DEFINING RETIREMENT

Words have power to shape our thinking. You don't want to "fall for" some of the dictionary definitions of retirement: "to withdraw, as for rest or shelter; to go to bed; to fall back; to retreat."

Even worse, for many people in previous generations retirement was "a brief period of time when you were too sick to work, but too well to die." That kind of thinking could poison your thinking about retirement, and your retirement life itself!

Instead, we need a new, more expansive definition that suggests a fun, abundant retirement life. Here are some ideas, many of which were offered by actual seminar participants and other mentors. Mark your favorites, then make your own definition using the elements that most appeal to you.

❑ When work is over...or at least optional.

❑ Time to pursue my passions.

❑ A new opportunity for self-actualization and chasing my dreams.

❑ Prosperous time.

❑ _____

_____

❑ *"The grandest of all life's adventures."* --*Mary Lloyd,* ***Supercharged Retirement***

- ❏ Life after required work.
- ❏ When I leave the rat-race and join the human race.
- ❏ *"Time to keep my promises." –Seminar participant*
- ❏ The Spanish word for retirement: *jubilación* ("jubilation"). Retiree: *jubilado* ("jubilant one"). Retirement age: *Edad de jubilación* ("age of jubilation").
- ❏ *"When I have enough…and I've had enough." –Seminar participant*
- ❏ Time to do what I want, when I want, with whomever I want.
- ❏ _____
  _____
- ❏ Time to live life livelier.
- ❏ Renaissance.
- ❏ *"Retirement may be looked upon either as a prolonged holiday or as a rejection, a being thrown on to the scrap-heap."*
  —Simone De Beauvoir
- ❏ _____
  _____
- ❏ Rebirth into the person I always wanted to be.
- ❏ Rebirth into the person I was always meant to be.
- ❏ *"Lose your title and find your life." –Bernice Bratter & Helen Dennis, **Project Renewment***
- ❏ The time to complete my growth.
- ❏ A mulligan.

- ❑ A time that is uniquely mine.
- ❑ Time to find myself.
- ❑ When work no longer gets in the way of what I really want to.

IN THEIR WORDS
Retirees tell it like it is

"This retirement stuff is the best life ever. I hope you get a chance to live it soon!"
--Retired attorney

- ❑ *"It's never too late to be what you might have been."* –novelist George Sand

- ❑ _____
  _____

- ❑ A time to rejoice, in life and in myself.
- ❑ A chance for a do-over.
- ❑ *"Retirement is wonderful. It's doing nothing without worrying about getting caught at it." —Gene Perret*
- ❑ A chance to do the kind of work I always wanted to, but could never afford.
- ❑ _____ every day! (Fill in the blank)
- ❑ When every week is six Saturdays and a Sunday.

- ❑ When every day is for vacation or vocation—whatever I choose.
- ❑ *"A second childhood without parental supervision."* – *Michael Stein,* **The Prosperous Retirement**
- ❑ Goodbye tension, hello pension!
- ❑ _____

  _____

- ❑ When you stop living at work and begin working at living.
- ❑ *"Retirement is the beginning of life, not the end."* —*Ernie J. Zelinski,* **How to Retire Happy, Wild, and Free**
- ❑ No Job, No Stress, No Pay!
- ❑ The time in your life when time is no longer money.
- ❑ The great escape.
- ❑ My metamorphosis, as a butterfly emerging from the cocoon.

CHAPTER TWO

GOODBYE WORK, HELLO RETIREMENT!

Starting your retirement journey starts with one step: out the door of the workplace. This can trigger an uplifting moment of liberation, or a difficult sense of loss. Welcome to retirement—one of life's major transitions. How will *you* deal with it?

Here are some thoughts on how the first days of retirement might be different from workdays, and how to tell when it's time to make the big move to retirement.

❑ *"To make an end is to make a beginning. The end is where we start from." –T.S. Eliot*

❑ Get up whenever I feel like it.

❑ Stay in touch with work friends.

❑ Turn off my alarm clock.

❑ Throw out my alarm clock.

❑ Throw my alarm clock as far as I can.

❑ "Dribble" my alarm clock like a basketball to see if it will bounce.

❑ Never have a boss again.

❑ _____
_____

❑ *"When is the right age to retire? When you dread going to work." —Mary Bright*

- ❑ Get up early to start another day of doing just what I want.

- ❑ *"The best day of your life is the one on which you decide your life is your own." –Bob Moawad*

- ❑ See what it's like to pursue activities for their own rewards, rather than being told what to do.

IN THEIR WORDS

Retirees tell it like it is

"We started retirement with a three-month trailer trip, like an extended vacation. By the time we got back, transition was a done deal."
--Retired manager

"I probably slowed down too much for the first few months. Then I perked up."
--Retiree

"It's true there's a transition time between work and retirement. Mine took about 20 seconds."
--Retired business manager

"I didn't want to be one of those people who retired without leaving the job."
--Retired college staffer

- ❑ Play "Take This Job and Shove It" at my retirement party.
- ❑ Discover the joy of being my own boss.
- ❑ Frame my last paycheck...or at least the pay stub.
- ❑ _____
  _____

IN THEIR WORDS
Retirees tell it like it is

"I _love_ doing everything slower—with no pressure!"
--Retiree after one month

"I still feel guilty if I'm not productive every day."
--Her friend, retired one year

- ❑ *"It is time I stepped aside for a less experienced and less able man." —Scott Elledge*
- ❑ Ignore the traffic reports at rush hour.
- ❑ Gloat over the traffic reports at rush hour.
- ❑ Sleep through rush hour.
- ❑ Learn about my pension options and exercise my wisdom in choosing.

- ❑ Finally find out what it's like to slow down to my own pace, instead of racing through every day.
- ❑ Visit my workplace in my "retirement clothes," just to rub it in.
- ❑ *"I can't change the direction of the wind, but I can adjust my sails to always reach my destination." –Jimmy Dean*
- ❑ See if there's a retirement club for fellow former employees of my workplace.
- ❑ _____
  _____

- ❑ *"Retire from work, but not from life." —M. K. Soni*
- ❑ Slow down and smell the flowers.
- ❑ Realize it's okay to miss my co-workers.
- ❑ _____
  _____

- ❑ Vow to not get "stuck" by only looking backward at the work life I left, but instead look forward to what comes next.
- ❑ *"Don't act your age [in retirement]. Act like the inner young person you have always been." —J. A. West*
- ❑ *"All transitions are composed of (1) an ending, (2) a neutral zone, and (3) a new beginning....change will happen—change is the norm now, and somehow or other we will need to develop ways of dealing productively with it. –William Bridges, **Transitions: Making Sense of Life's Changes***

❑ Grab some poster board, scissors, glue stick, and a stack of old magazines to create my "retirement vision board"—a collage of words, phrases, and pictures that represent my ideal retirement—and then live it.

IN THEIR WORDS
Retirees tell it like it is

"Leaving work, I felt this huge weight come off my shoulders. I didn't even know it was there before."
--Retired department manager

"I knew I was ready to retire because it was harder to care anymore."
--Retired college administrator

"I knew I was ready to retire because it wasn't fun, and I didn't like the person I had become."
--Retired college professor

"Now I'm in complete control of my schedule. I don't do _anything_ I don't want to."
--Retiree

- ❏ Realize that I have a lifetime of transitions behind me, so this one will be familiar, but with more wisdom.
- ❏ Watch the sunset, the whole show, from sundown to first stars.
- ❏ Aim for a retirement where there's a mix of education, work, and leisure ("learning, earning, and burning") every year.
- ❏ _____
  _____
- ❏ *"The future belongs to those who believe in the beauty of their dreams." —Eleanor Roosevelt*
- ❏ Recognize that I miss the sense of purpose I always had at work, and start to develop a new retirement purpose.
- ❏ Align my retirement vision with my key strengths and values by working with the book, *What Color Is Your Parachute For Retirement,* by John Nelson and Richard Bolles.
- ❏ *"The best time to start thinking about your retirement is before your boss does." —Unknown wise person*
- ❏ _____
  _____
- ❏ *"He who is not ready today will be less so tomorrow." –Ovid*
- ❏ Celebrate that my retirement might be just as long as my career—with all the opportunities for growth and learning.
- ❏ *"Retirement to me does not mean nothing to do but the realization of the decisions I made in the past. That I made in my life." —Jack Bowman*

- ☐ Ask, "Am I still needed the way I was at work?"
- ☐ Bask in the luxury of slowing down a notch.
- ☐ Consider working with a personal coach to help me design my ideal retirement life. See "General Retirement" in the "Resources" chapter.

NOTES

CHAPTER THREE

LOCATION, LOCATION, LOCATION
HOUSING CHOICES

Where will you retire? Where will your retirement dreams play out?

Research shows that only a small minority of retirees move in retirement. Even fewer change their state or province of residence. It seems that many pre-retirees think they will move, but end up staying in their pre-retirement homes.

So look around your home and your home town, with an eye to maximizing your retirement health, safety and opportunities.

But also consider the wealth of relocation opportunities, again with the aim of making your retirement life the best it can be. You might consider moving to be closer to your planned retirement activities, or to be near the people you value most, or to say "goodbye and good riddance" to home and yard maintenance. Just remember, moving can mean finding new doctors, dentists, friends, and a lawyer to help you redraft your estate plan.

Here are some ideas to spark your thinking about your retirement location and housing.

❑ Get rid of the big family manse to make housecleaning a breeze.

❑ Downsize and invest the difference in cost.

❑ Check out secure senior communities with the clubhouse, pool, gardens, walking trails, and other amenities.

- ❏ Give mobile home living a go.
- ❏ Finally leave the noisy, go-go city and try country living.
- ❏ Move into town where everything is an easy walk away.
- ❏ Consider a condo for easy maintenance and lower purchase price.
- ❏ _____
  _____

IN THEIR WORDS
Retirees tell it like it is

"I got a new roof, furnace, and kitchen appliances before I retired, while I still had a paycheck. I gave myself 25 years of carefree housing. And it was a great excuse to re-do the kitchen."
--Retired counselor

- ❏ Realize that my need for privacy or loud music dictate my own four walls—a single family home.
- ❏ Make sure that wherever I am, I can pursue my love of gardening—even if it's just containers on the deck.
- ❏ Move closer to the kids and grandkids.
- ❏ Move far, far away from the kids and grandkids.
- ❏ Make sure that my housing choice will accommodate big family gatherings.

- ❑ Make sure that my housing choice will *not* accommodate "boomerang" kids (that keep coming back to live).

- ❑ Give my home a thorough safety review—and fix any shortcomings. See the Housing Safety Checklist at *www.ces.ncsu.edu/depts/fcs/pdfs/FCS-461.pdf.*

- ❑ _____
  _____

- ❑ Compare the monthly condo fees in my area to putting the same amount into "hiring out" all the maintenance on my single-family home. It might make more sense to stay put and pay someone to take care of the house and yard.

- ❑ Live near the activities I love.

- ❑ Live where I feel the most whole—in the mountains, in a forest, among open fields, or at the shore.

- ❑ Sell it all and hit the road full-time. See *www.rv-dreams.com* and *www.fulltimervliving.net.*

- ❑ _____
  _____

- ❑ Join the "tiny houses" movement, placed either on my own land or that of friend or family. See *www.designboom.com/contemporary/tiny_houses.html* and/or *www.smallhousestyle.com.*

- ❑ Just say no to ownership! Carefree apartment living for me.

- ❑ "Snowbird" between my summer and winter retirement homes.

- ❑ Make the big move to overseas living. See *http://internationalliving.com.*

- ❑ Sell my principal residence and move full-time to my vacation home.

- ❑ Live on a golf course.

- ❑ Expand my horizons by living with a view.

- ❑ _____

  _____

- ❑ Convert the kids' old bedrooms into spaces for my new retirement life: exercise room, office, craft room, art studio....

- ❑ Make sure that where I choose to live can support me as I age—with medical services, transportation, and personal care.

- ❑ Go beyond the "fix-it" list and make home improvement my retirement mission.

- ❑ Make my home a retirement sanctuary.

- ❑ Think of my home as the "mother ship" that launches and grounds all my retirement adventures.

- ❑ Crime-proof my home for retirement peace of mind. (Remember, most burglars gain entrance through an unlocked door.)

- ❑ Consider the direction my neighborhood is headed—will it still be a good retirement area in ten years? Twenty?

- ❑ Look into "pocket neighborhoods"—small clusters of smaller homes, grouped around a courtyard or walking mall. See Pocket Neighborhoods book entry in the Resources chapter.

❏ As I consider a new location, make sure I know all its moods in all four seasons.

❏ _____

_____

❏ Live full-time in my favorite vacation destination.

❏ If I plan to move, don't sell my home prematurely. Keep it as an "undo" return option for a year or more. Maybe rent it out to cover ownership expenses.

❏ Pay off the house for peace of mind and affordable living.

❏ Live on a boat and pull up anchor any time I want a change of scenery.

❏ Look for a condo or neighborhood with an extensive Pea Patch shared garden.

NOTES

CHAPTER FOUR

RIGHT ON THE MONEY
DOLLARS AND SENSE

Planning your retirement finances is all-important—before you retire. The number one concern of *pre*-retirees is the money. But once retired, most people report that they think about the money a lot less—it is what it is and you live within it. Instead, retirees are more concerned with lifestyle—what to do and who to do it with.

Finances and lifestyle are intertwined. Everything has a price tag. It's wise to think ahead to be sure your retirement dreams are affordable and your retirement finances are sustainable. Whether you work with pencil and paper, your own spreadsheets, on-line calculators, or a professional financial planner, you need to make sure the numbers work. Here are ideas to move you forward on your financial planning.

❑ Contact my employer or union to check my pension rights and payout options.

❑ Contact Social Security at *www.ssa.gov*, (800) SSA-1213, or my local office, to determine when and how to start my payments. (Shameless promotion: check Amazon for the latest edition of *Social Security, The Inside Story* by Andy Landis.)

❑ *"Live big. It's about the size of your life, not the size of your wallet." –Dr. David Yeske, CFP*

- ❑ Peruse "Find a Planner" *www.fpanet.org* to learn about financial planners...including how to choose one.

- ❑ Look for a "fee-only" financial planner in my area at *www.napfa.org*.

- ❑ *"Annual income 20 pounds, annual expenditure 19 and 6, result happiness. Annual income 20 pounds, annual expenditure 20 pounds ought and 6, result misery." – Charles Dickens*

- ❑ _____
_____

- ❑ Check *www.moneyquotient.org* to see if there's a "Financial Life Planner" in my area (one who holistically integrates my finances with my life values and goals).

- ❑ Get a quick financial "tune-up" by hiring a financial planner "by the hour" through *www.garrettplanningnetwork.com*.

- ❑ Read "The Ultimate Buy-and-Hold Strategy" at *www.merriman.com/PDFs/UltimateBuyAndHold.pdf*. (Search *www.merriman.com* for the latest version.)

- ❑ *"Measure wealth not by the things you have, but by the things you have for which you would not take money." – Unknown*

- ❑ Stop looking at the stock market every day...or even every week.

- ❑ Look into an immediate annuity—basically buying my own pension on my own terms (like survivor benefits or inflation protection)—to ensure I never outlive my money. (See *www.immediateannuities.com* for information and quotes.)

IN THEIR WORDS
Retirees tell it like it is

"We worried about the money a lot, before retirement. I made spreadsheets, all kind of projections, and met with financial planners. But once you retire, you find out in the first few months what you have, and you just live on it."
--Retiree

"I figured out how much I would have to live on in retirement. Then I actually lived on that much for one year before I retired, to be sure it would work. Now that I'm retired I'm living on even less."
--Retired college administrator

"I'm on a tight budget. But I tell myself that the paychecks I no longer get are buying time, rather than goods and services."
--Retired college professor

❑ Check the administrative cost of my mutual funds and research ways to get similar returns with lower fees.

❑ Give up on investment gimmicks and focus on a broadly diversified portfolio that I rebalance periodically.

- ❑ Make investing simple—at last.

- ❑ _____

  _____

- ❑ Calculate my retirement "number"—the amount I need to save—with the Ballpark Estimator at *www.choosetosave.org/ballpark/*.

- ❑ *"In spite of the cost of living, it's still popular." –Kathleen Norris*

- ❑ Eliminate emotional swings from my investing decisions.

- ❑ Carefully and wisely plan how much I can withdraw from savings each year so I don't outlive my money.

- ❑ Assess my savings readiness with a computer estimator like Vanguard's excellent, graphical "Retirement Income Calculator" at *https://retirementplans.vanguard.com/VGApp/pe/ pubeducation/calculators/RetirementIncomeCalc.jsf*. Compare results with AARP's "Nest Egg Calculator" at *www.aarp.org/Retirement_Calculator*.

- ❑ _____

  _____

- ❑ Check at *www.irs.gov/pub/irs-pdf/f1040es.pdf* to see if I need to file quarterly estimated taxes, now that my paycheck will be stopping. (Search *www.irs.gov* for "1040 ES" for the latest instructions.)

- ❑ *"Don't focus on the money. Instead, ask yourself what is the experience you want most in your life." –James Weil*

- ❑ Run my retirement income picture past a tax professional, just in case.

- ❏ Contact IRS at *www.irs.gov*, (800) 829-1040, or a local IRS office to see how my tax situation might change with my retirement.

- ❏ *"Retirement is like a long vacation in Las Vegas. The goal is to enjoy it the fullest, but not so fully that you run out of money." —Jonathan Clements*

- ❏ _____
  _____

- ❏ Learn about Required Minimum Distributions from my traditional IRA as I approach age 70-1/2.

- ❏ Learn how to use my Roth IRA to avoid higher tax brackets.

- ❏ *"The question isn't at what age I want to retire, it's at what income." —George Foreman*

- ❏ Explore "charitable remainder trusts" that give me income and a tax break now, and benefits to my charities later.

- ❏ Use strategic withdrawals from my Roth IRA to avoid taxation of my Social Security benefits.

- ❏ _____
  _____

- ❏ Automate withdrawals and rebalancing so I can get on with the important things in life—like living!

- ❏ Talk with a mortgage professional to see exactly what I would have to pay each month to "retire" the mortgage on my retirement date.

- ❏ See how quickly I can achieve debt-free living in retirement (if not before).

- ❑ Separate my bills into "needs" (like housing, utilities, and food) and "nice-to-haves" (like vacations, cable TV, and entertainment). Then make sure that my "needs" list can be covered with certain or near-certain income like Social Security, pension, immediate annuities, or interest income. The "nice-to-haves" list can be covered by at-risk income.

- ❑ _____
  _____

- ❑ *"Money is something you got to make in case you don't die."*
  —Max Asnas

- ❑ Consider Long-Term Care (LTC) insurance to protect against a potentially devastating financial burden. The non-biased booklet "A Shopper's Guide to Long-Term Care Insurance" can be ordered for free at *https://eapps.naic.org/forms/ipsd/Consumer_info.jsp*.

- ❑ See if a reverse mortgage—where the mortgage company pays me or gives me a line of credit—is for me. See *www.ftc.gov/bcp/edu/pubs/consumer/homes/rea13.shtm*.

- ❑ _____
  _____

- ❑ Protect my assets by avoiding scams and identity theft. See *www.ftc.gov/idtheft* and *www.fbi.gov/scams-safety/fraud/ seniors*.

- ❑ Consider the many ways to tap into my home equity, including downsizing and investing the difference.

- ❑ Bite the bullet and face the fact that I need to delay retirement until the numbers pencil out better.

❑ Always maintain a positive attitude and a positive cash flow.

❑ Regularly practice the following phrase: "Do you offer a senior discount?"

NOTES

CHAPTER FIVE

ESTATE PLANNING
AND MY GREATER LEGACY

Estate planning is about a lot more than the (inevitable) death and taxes. It also deals with these questions:

- If I'm away on a long vacation, who will pay my bills?
- If I'm in an auto accident and unconscious, who can authorize medical care?
- How can I make sure my affairs are handled with maximum ease and minimum expense?
- How can I be a peace-maker, and avoid a painful rift that could divide the family forever?

In short, your estate plan should bolster your legal status in retirement, and also your psychological well-being.

Estate planning is also about a lot more than your "stuff." It's about communicating your deepest values and your love to those most important to you.

Here are some thoughts to make your legacy planning thorough, accurate, and caring.

❑ Hire an estate planning attorney so a professional is helping me put all my affairs in order.

❑ Carefully study my favorite charities to see which ones should be remembered in my will.

- ❑ Include all the kids in my will, no matter how they've wronged me, so I can be remembered as a "peace-maker" rather than a vengeful parent.

- ❑ _____
  _____

- ❑ Take responsibility for my affairs rather than leave a mess for someone to try and clean up.

- ❑ Realize that my legacy is much more than money, and create an "ethical will" using Susan Turnbull's *The Wealth of Your Life,* to communicate my deepest values to the next generation. (See "Resources" chapter)

- ❑ Make an audio or video record of my fondest memories.

- ❑ Make sure I have the "must-have" documents for estate planning: a Will and/or Revocable Trust, a Durable Power of Attorney for Financial Matters, a Durable Power of Attorney for Health Care, and a Health Care Directive ("Living Will").

- ❑ _____
  _____

- ❑ Make sure my assets are properly titled (e.g. sole ownership, joint ownership, joint tenancy with right of survivorship, etc.), in line with my wishes. (The type of titling can "trump" the will.)

- ❑ On accounts with beneficiary designations (life insurance, IRAs, 401(k)s, annuities, etc.), check the named beneficiaries to be sure they align with my wishes and the rest of the estate plan. (Beneficiary designations can "trump" the will.)

- ❑ Make arrangements for the disability of a spouse or other family member.
- ❑ Check the estate plan to see if it's current. Has there been a birth, death, marriage, divorce, or change in the laws— or in my wishes?
- ❑ _____
  _____

- ❑ Explore how my estate plan would handle the need for long-term care (e.g. a nursing home stay).
- ❑ Spend time with older people to learn from their experiences and wisdom.
- ❑ Resist the sales pitches for packaged "Living Trusts," which may or may not be right for me.
- ❑ Avoid the temptation to make a home-made will online, without talking to an attorney.
- ❑ Make sure any "special needs" heirs in my will—like those with legal incompetency or other disabilities— receive appropriate trust protection or other legal arrangements.
- ❑ _____
  _____

- ❑ Schedule a meeting with a "planned giving" coordinator at my favorite charity.
- ❑ If I have an heir with wayward ways (drugs, alcohol, etc.), learn how to use the estate plan to guide them to recovery.
- ❑ Provide for my place of worship in my will.

- [ ] Carefully consider my end-of-life wishes, and record them in my Health Care Directive ("Living Will").

- [ ] _____

- [ ] Call a family meeting to discuss my estate arrangements with those concerned, omitting any specific dollar amounts.

- [ ] Check with my preferred estate administrator ("executor") before I make it official in the documents.

- [ ] Start a conversation with my loved ones about my "five wishes" for final care. See *www.caringinfo.org* and/or *www.agingwithdignity.org/five-wishes.php.*

- [ ] *"Everyone gets organized at some point, they just might not be around for it." —Sue DeRoos*

- [ ] _____

- [ ] Ask friends, "Who knows a good estate planning attorney?" to find the right professional.

- [ ] Communicate your wishes, the location of your vital papers, and the names of your advisors, with a "Family Love Letter." See *www.FamilyLoveLetter.com.*

- [ ] _____

- [ ] Find a fair way to distribute the "little things" with low economic value but enormous emotional value. (See *How to Divide Your Family's Estate and Heirlooms Peacefully and Sensibly* and *Who Gets Grandma's Yellow Pie Plate? Workbook* in the "Resources" chapter.)

❑ Reduce my legal fees by learning all I can about estate planning before the attorney starts the clock running.

❑ Schedule an appointment now to get the ball rolling.

NOTES

CHAPTER SIX

RELATIONSHIPS: MY SPOUSE/PARTNER

The next three chapters raise the question: Who will be part of your retirement life? What relationships will be altered when you retire?

The one person you will spend the most retirement time with is your spouse, partner, or best friend. That much togetherness is a huge shift in the relationship, and can be a blessing or a strain.

During work years you can get by with a "maintenance" relationship: saying hello, saying goodbye, a peck on the cheek, check the shopping list, a note to say you'll be late. That won't cut it when you're thrown together 24/7, or when one of you is retired and the other is still at work.

We've all heard the (bitter) jokes: "I've got half the money and twice the husband." "We married for better or worse, but not for breakfast, lunch, and dinner." Indeed, some couples can't adjust to the changes and end up drifting apart, or worse.

Retirement will mean a re-negotiation of the relationship. Solutions you find will be unique to you—every couple is different—but in time you might discover a deeper, richer relationship than you ever had before. Communication is key.

On the other hand, retirement may mean a search for that special someone. Here are some ideas to get started:

❑ Honor my partner's need for space and privacy.

- ❑ Support my partner's own retirement or work pursuits.
- ❑ Find a partner to share retirement adventures.
- ❑ _____
  _____

IN THEIR WORDS
Retirees tell it like it is

"Who is this stranger who moved into my house?"
--Neighbor "Pat," after her husband retired

"I never realized until my husband retired that our house is too small. But when he started spending every day watching Perry Mason re-runs and playing solitaire, I wanted a much bigger house."
--Neighbor

"We're loving the time together. We're falling in love all over again."
--Couple in a retiree panel

- ❑ Find out what my partner really wants to do...and join in.
- ❑ Dance the night away.
- ❑ Communicate my retirement dreams and concerns to my partner.

❑ Find my soul mate participating in the same activities I love.

IN THEIR WORDS

Retirees tell it like it is

"We knew we needed a lot of 'space' for our own pursuits, so we built the house in two wings, with her stuff in one wing, my stuff in the other, and the kitchen in the middle. My plan was to have breakfast together, go do my own thing, get together for lunch, go do my own thing, and have dinner together. The plan lasted one day. On Day Two I packed my lunch!"
--Retired civil engineer

"It's like a second honeymoon, with wisdom."
--Married retiree

"After I was widowed my sister set me up for a date with a nice gentleman. At dinner he confided, 'I know you have concerns, so you should know: I have my own Long-Term Care insurance.' The next day I told my sister, 'Well, their line sure has changed since we were young!'"
--Retired counselor

- ❏ Honor the "honey-do" list…within reason.
- ❏ _____
  _____
- ❏ Listen and discover who my partner really is.
- ❏ Vow never to drive my partner bonkers. Distracted, yes, but bonkers, no.
- ❏ _____
  _____
- ❏ Make a deal to avoid growing apart in retirement.
- ❏ Give my valentine a personalized romance novel starring the two of us. See *www.yournovel.com* or *www.bookbyyou.com*.
- ❏ Do everything in my power to nurture our relationship as we transition into retirement.
- ❏ Share with my partner a private feeling I've had about my retirement.
- ❏ Talk to a counselor or clergyman about making these the best years of our relationship.
- ❏ Renew my vows.
- ❏ Create new vows together.
- ❏ *"The good life means living in the place where you belong, being with people you love, doing the right work—on purpose." —Richard Leider*
- ❏ _____
  _____
- ❏ Listen to my partner's retirement dreams and concerns.

- ❏ Sign up for online dating—with honesty.
- ❏ Discover new activities and people that we can share in retirement together.
- ❏ Work out our issues before we're thrown together 24/7.
- ❏ _____
  _____
- ❏ Think about how we relate on vacations together for insight into what might work best in retirement.
- ❏ With all the extra time to grow our relationship, who knows what amorous activities might happen on some mornings or afternoons?

NOTES

CHAPTER SEVEN

RELATIONSHIPS:
KINSHIP
MY FAMILY, KIDS, AND GRANDKIDS

Retirement will have a dramatic impact on all your relationships, including your family ties.

The gift of time in retirement allows for deepening your family relationships more than your work years allowed. But that same gift of time can make family members think you have nothing to do, tempting them to impose their needs on your hard-earned retirement life. In some cases they might grow to resent your "life of ease," and pull away from you.

These issues can be worked out. Enjoy your family in new and deeper ways, on your terms. The key is communicating your retirement hopes and concerns to your loved ones, preferably well before you retire. There are many ways to bring joy to your family ties:

❑ Spoil the grandkids.

❑ Host an annual family get-together at a new attraction every year.

❑ Get to know the grandkids in a way I never had time to do with my own kids.

❑ _____
   _____

- ❏ Remember to give the gifts of time and care to my parents, if living.
- ❏ Host everyone on a Disney cruise.
- ❏ Build a complete collection of my favorite children's books, then let the grandkids pick a title a day for reading aloud together.
- ❏ Get re-acquainted with my brothers and sisters.
- ❏ Make a point of taking the kids or grandkids out to the movie they're raving about.
- ❏ _____
  _____

- ❏ *"Time is the coin of your life. It is the only coin you have, and only you can determine how it will be spent. Be careful lest you let other people spend it for you." —Carl Sandburg*
- ❏ Make my place a home-away-from-home for the grandkids.
- ❏ Live near my kids and grandkids.
- ❏ Make a point of not living "too" near to the kids and grandkids.
- ❏ Take Mom to lunch and shopping.
- ❏ Tell the kids I'd love to offer "grandparent daycare" –and then suggest the right number of days per week that suit me.
- ❏ _____
  _____

- ❏ Institute "home-cooking" day at my place.
- ❏ Make sure I have a big enough car to haul the grandkids.

- ❑ Spoil the grandkids with experiences, not things.
- ❑ Stage a snowball shootout.

- ❑ Explore the "Family Programs" offered by Road Scholar (formerly Elderhostel), designed for two or more generations of my family to learn and experience together. See *www.roadscholar.org/programs/familyprograms.asp.*
- ❑ Take the grandkids on an old-fashioned driving vacation—well, maybe a short one to start.

- ❏ Find your favorite family picture and have it made into a jigsaw puzzle, mug, or calendar for the youngsters.
- ❏ Take a class together.
- ❏ Build a snow grandparent and grandchild.
- ❏ Introduce the grandkids to classical music at a youth orchestra concert.
- ❏ Horse around at the circus.
- ❏ _____

- ❏ Take Dad on the next family vacation.
- ❏ *"Human beings are the only creatures on earth that allow their children to come back home." —Bill Cosby*
- ❏ Monkey around at the zoo.
- ❏ Volunteer to drive the grandkids to their after-school activities for a week.
- ❏ Get in the swim at the aquarium.
- ❏ _____

- ❏ Take the grandkids to a local lecture on whatever drives them wild—dinosaurs, airplanes, doll history, whatever.
- ❏ Give your kids "adult time" by taking the grandkids overnight to a local hotel...with a pool, of course.
- ❏ Volunteer to participate in a school video or audio project about life in "the old days."
- ❏ Volunteer to write the checks for all my parents' bills, and prepare a single itemized bill for reimbursement.

- ❑ Give the grandkids the gift of time.
- ❑ Communicate clearly to everyone in the family my vision for family time in my retirement.
- ❑ _____
  _____

- ❑ Teach the grandkids how to camp.
- ❑ Take a walk in the park with a stop at the playground.
- ❑ Tell the kids tactfully you can't accommodate their returning home to live.
- ❑ Tell the kids they're always welcome to live at your home, if needed.
- ❑ _____
  _____

- ❑ Schedule a professional multi-generational family portrait.
- ❑ Take everybody to the roller-skating (or ice-skating) rink.
- ❑ Listen to my kids' concerns, without offering solutions.
- ❑ Get the whole family on Facebook.
- ❑ Take the grandkids out for a free or nearly free meal! Research at *www.kidseatfreeplaces.com.*

NOTES

CHAPTER EIGHT

RELATIONSHIPS: MY SOCIAL CIRCLE

Will retirement affect your social contacts? Count on it.

Think about it: most of the "people time" you have in your working years happens in the workplace. When you no longer spend your days there, how will you avoid becoming a hermit?

For us guys, our default position is to go it alone or make our spouse/partner our entire support group. Neither approach works well. "Alone" feels like "lonely" very quickly, and we will drive our partner crazy—and away—if all our people contact goes through them.

Many women are surprised how much of their support group is at work. That changes at retirement.

Meanwhile, many of your non-work friends are still at *their* work five days a week, not available for socializing, and might even feel a little resentful at your new-found freedom.

The reality is that you'll stay in touch with some work friends. You'll maintain your non-work friendships. And you'll find new friends that fit with your emerging retirement life, probably through your retirement activities. But it will all be different from the past. Here are some ideas for quality social time:

❑ Schedule a brunch with friends.

❑ Join the "regulars" at my local diner, until the waitress greets my friends and me by name.

- ❏ Next time I engage in my favorite activity, invite someone I meet to coffee.
- ❏ Follow Stephen Covey's advice to "seek first to understand, then to be understood."
- ❏ _____
_____
- ❏ Next time I engage in my favorite activity, invite a friend to come along.
- ❏ Join a service organization like Elks, Lions, or Rotary.
- ❏ Invite an old friend to coffee.
- ❏ Go to a reunion and see if I recognize classmates—and if they recognize me.
- ❏ Volunteer to help a friend after surgery.
- ❏ Meet the neighbors.
- ❏ Start a block-watch group.
- ❏ Take a meal to someone who's ill.
- ❏ Join a wine-tasting club.
- ❏ Share a secret.
- ❏ Ask some neighbors to join me in a trash pickup walk.
- ❏ Give someone the gift of giving: say "yes" when they ask if there's anything they can do for you.
- ❏ Chat with someone I don't know over coffee at my place of worship.
- ❏ Look for new friends at my volunteer activity.
- ❏ Strike up a conversation with someone at the bookstore or library.

- [ ] Be friendly.
- [ ] _____

_____

- [ ] Get back in touch with old friends.
- [ ] Add some Facebook friends.
- [ ] Say hi to a fellow neighborhood walker.
- [ ] Share my family photos with a new acquaintance.
- [ ] Ask, "How are you—really?" and listen to the answer.
- [ ] Greet the folks at the next table at the restaurant.
- [ ] Smile more.
- [ ] Invite my friends and neighbors over for a backyard barbeque.
- [ ] Start a neighborhood book exchange. Web-search for several sites, including www.obseussed.com/2012/06/start-neighborhood-book-exchange.html.
- [ ] Join www.meetup.com to discover a universe of social activities near me in my areas of interest.

NOTES

CHAPTER NINE

RETIREMENT ACTIVITIES
TRY IT!
THINGS TO TRY IN RETIREMENT

Now is the time to think about what you will *do* with all the time released when you retire. You probably devote 50-60 hours (or more!) per week to your work, if you include dressing, commuting, and all the other prep time for work. At retirement, all those hours—over 2500 hours per year—are handed to you, empty.

That's too much time to fritter away in meaningless activities. You'll go bananas with too much "down time," but you don't want to overfill your calendar either.

You'll find that you're in charge of everything about your retirement activities:

- their *quantity* (how busy or free you are),
- their *quality* (how fulfilling and engaging they are), and
- their *variety* (how you build a mix of different activities).

At the beginning, anything goes. What do you *want* to do? What sounds *fun?* This chapter and the next six give you some ideas to get your thinking started:

❑ Do something I've always dreamed of doing.

❑ Create a "bucket list"—must-dos before I kick the bucket—and start checking off the items.

- ❑ *"A great pleasure in life is doing what people say you cannot do." —Walter Gagehot*

- ❑ Think back to the activities I loved the most over the years, and "re-do" some favorites...this time with the experience of a lifetime.

- ❑ _____
  _____

- ❑ *"Don't simply retire from something; have something to retire to." —Harry Emerson Fosdick*

- ❑ Tackle the fix-it list around my place.

- ❑ Take charge of the quantity of retirement activities, so I'm in the comfort zone of "not too busy, not too idle."

- ❑ *"The key to retirement is to find joy in the little things." –Susan Miller*

- ❑ Drive a race car.

- ❑ Live the maxim that "anything worth doing is worth doing poorly," so I don't limit myself to only those activities I've already mastered.

- ❑ *"We have no porch, no rocking chair—and no time. My biggest need is a calendar because there are so many things to do. Now I encourage people to retire—the younger the better." —Maurice Musholt*

- ❑ Get the mess in the basement/garage/storage room cleaned out and organized.

- ❑ Finally get into boating.

- ❏ Start a vegetable garden and dine healthy on the fruits of my labors.
- ❏ Get the hang of hang-gliding.
- ❏ _____
  _____
- ❏ *"Go confidently in the direction of your dreams! Live the life you've imagined." --Henry David Thoreau*
- ❏ Take charge of the quality of retirement activities, so I'm involved with meaningful activities, not busy-work.
- ❏ Remember that I can rent anything—boats, cars, RVs, and vacation cottages—without the hassle and expense of owning.
- ❏ *"A perpetual holiday is a good working definition of hell."* —*George Bernard Shaw*
- ❏ Take to the skies with paragliding, the flying sport where the entire aircraft fits in a backpack.
- ❏ Join the buzz on backyard bee-keeping.
- ❏ Give myself permission to fail, so I keep trying new things.
- ❏ *"Half our life is spent trying to find something to do with the time we have rushed through life trying to save."* —*Will Rogers*
- ❏ Leap into a sky-diving class.
- ❏ Rock out at electric guitar lessons.
- ❏ _____
  _____
- ❏ Mount up and power into (safe) motorcycling.

- ❏ *"Make no mistake that you have a dream, and that your dream seeks expression. Your dream will not rest until you give it some exposure in your life." —Richard Johnson*

- ❏ Build some variety into my retirement activities to keep it interesting: some social, some solo; some active, some quiet; some physical, some mental or emotional.

- ❏ Start a jazz band.

- ❏ *"If you can dream it, you can do it." —Walt Disney*

- ❏ Improve my horsemanship.

- ❏ Time my activities for the weekdays, when most people are at work, leaving all the leisure goodies to us retirees.

- ❏ *Either you let your life slip away by not doing the things you want to do, or you get up and do them. —Roger Von Oech*

- ❏ _____
  _____

- ❏ Get the car I always wanted but couldn't afford, restore it, and cruise the local burger joint.

- ❏ Discover geocaching, the worldwide hobby that combines high-tech with outdoors activity. See *www.geocaching.com*.

- ❏ Make sure my library card is up-to-date, because I plan to do a lot of reading—just like Sunday afternoon, but any day of the week.

- ❏ Find just the right mix of productive work (paid or unpaid), learning, and leisure time.

- *"Some mistakes are too much fun to only make once."* — *Brad Paisley*
- Follow the advice of Lord Chesterfield: "Whatever is worth doing at all is worth doing well."

IN THEIR WORDS
Retirees tell it like it is

"I'm not concerned about boredom. Boredom can be preparation for what's next."
--Retired college professor

"Everybody says you're not supposed to do this, but I'm really enjoying 'riding the La-Z-boy.' My wife keeps trying to get me to get out and do things—she's selling real estate & water skiing & and a lot else—but I'm enjoying resting up. Of course, I have to take the boat out every morning to drag her [BLEEP] around the lake."
--Retired manager

- *"Chase your passion, not your pension."* —*Denis Waitley*
- Drop in on a senior center to see what's going on.
- If I don't like the first senior center I visit, I'll try a different one.

❑ *"We do not stop playing because we are old, we grow old because we stop playing." —Variously attributed to Oliver Wendell Holmes, Benjamin Franklin, George Bernard Shaw, and others.*

❑ _____
_____

❑ Turn on with autocross racing—like a miniature road course laid out on a parking lot, for safe, amateur competition using any smaller car. Or just go as a spectator for free. Web-search "autocross" for local clubs and events

❑ Amaze myself with the new things I try and the new "me" I become.

❑ *"Even if you're on the right track, you'll get run over if you just sit there." —Will Rogers*

❑ Run for local office. Or state office. Or national office.

❑ _____
_____

❑ Have fun behind the wheel with auto rallying—either "gimmick," with fun clues and puzzles to solve on the route, or "Time-Speed-Distance," using precision driving to stay as close as possible to a mathematically perfect time on course. Any car will do (the author started with his mom's 1964 Pontiac station wagon). Web-search "auto rally" or "auto rallye" for local clubs and events.

❑ Start a neighborhood website.

❑ Take pilot's lessons and fly an airplane solo.

- ❑ *"Life's not about expecting, hoping and wishing, it's about doing, being and becoming. It's about the choices you've just made, and the ones you're about to make, it's about the things you choose to say—today. It's about what you're gonna do after you finish reading this."* —*Mike Dooley*

- ❑ Gee, I always wanted to get into the hobby of radio-controlled airplanes...or cars...or boats...or helicopters....

- ❑ Whatever I do, remember there's probably a club or association affiliated with it, for more fun and social contact.

NOTES

CHAPTER TEN

RETIREMENT ACTIVITIES
TOUR IT
RETIREMENT TRAVEL

In seminar after seminar, participants list "travel" near the top of their retirement dreams. An aura of adventure, exploration, and discovery surrounds it. Even those who travel regularly for work aspire to leisure travel in retirement.

Travel means different things to different people. For one it might mean a car trip with tent camping; for another, jetting overseas and staying in five-star hotels; and for yet another, a relaxing cruise. Even those on a tighter budget might plan a bigger trip once every year or two, or for a special occasion.

Whatever your travel budget, consider these ideas, or limber up your imagination to plan travel that will be truly memorable:

❑ Find out if all my friends are right about going on a cruise.

❑ Drive across the country both ways in a big circle, visiting every national park within reach.

❑ Read and study Patricia Schultz's book, *1,000 Places to See Before Your Die,* for 1,000 travel ideas.

❑ Drive to Alaska.

❑ _____

_____

- ❑ Travel to my favorite place and stay there for a month. Or two. Or three.
- ❑ Cruise Antarctica and commune with the penguins.
- ❑ Visit every English-speaking island in the tropics.
- ❑ Save money on travel by getting a city pass or country pass, good for multiple attractions.
- ❑ Take a float plane to a remote fishing spot.
- ❑ _____
  _____

- ❑ Mush a dogsled.
- ❑ Fly around the world on one of those Round The World (RTW) tickets: _http://wikitravel.org/en/Round_the_world_flights_
- ❑ Drive onto the Alaska Ferry (you can board in Bellingham, Washington), cruise the Inside Passage, and drive off to explore the 49th State.
- ❑ Take the laptop with me on my travels so I can frequently Skype and Facebook with the kids and grandkids.
- ❑ _"Twenty years from now you will be more disappointed by the things you didn't do than by the ones you did do. So throw off the bowlines, sail away from the safe harbor, and catch the trade winds in your sails. Explore. Dream. Discover." —Mark Twain_
- ❑ _____
  _____

- ❑ Get a list of all national parks and start checking them off.
- ❑ Drive to the tip of South America.

- ❑ Ride a bobsled at 60 mph.
- ❑ Spin the globe, stab a spot, learn the language, book the trip.
- ❑ Spend the night as a "keeper" at a remote lighthouse. (See *www.uslhs.org/resources_be_a_keeper.php*.)
- ❑ Make my travel dreams affordable with home exchange, anywhere in the world. See *www.homeexchange.com*.

IN THEIR WORDS
Retirees tell it like it is

"I wanted to travel the world. My wife hates to travel. So I traveled with each of my kids, one at a time—wherever in the world they wanted to go."
--Retired nuclear engineer

- ❑ _____
  _____

- ❑ Soak it up with a European "kur" (cure) vacation, travelling from spa to spa. (Web-search "kur vacation.")
- ❑ Exercise the exchange rights on my vacation timeshare to travel the world, two weeks at a time.
- ❑ Feed my soul in the world's sacred places with "spiritual travel" or "pilgrimage." See *www.spiritquesttours.com* or *www.divinetravels.com*.

- ☐ Share my travels with the whole family via social networking on the computer.

- ☐ Explore the sister cities of my home town.

- ☐ _____

  _____

- ☐ Live in a rural French farmhouse through the "Gites" program. See *http://en.gites-de-france.com.*

- ☐ Tour every baseball park in the U.S., grab some peanuts, and stay for the game.

- ☐ Get a travel pass for my destination country (e.g. Eurail pass) and see where it takes me.

- ☐ Visit every U.S. state and/or every Canadian province.

- ☐ Travel to the country of my birth (or of my ancestors) and learn about family lore.

- ☐ Visit every country in North and South America.

- ☐ Buy an "America the Beautiful" pass ($10 at press-time for those 62 and over) for lifetime free access to National Parks and recreation sites, and many amenities. See *http://www.nps.gov/findapark/passes.htm.*

- ☐ Arrange a free walking tour of my destination town, led by a proud local. Web-search "free walking tours" plus the destination city. (The guide will probably appreciate a tip.)

CHAPTER ELEVEN

RETIREMENT ACTIVITIES
LEARN IT
LIFELONG EDUCATION

Retirement offers a tremendous opportunity for adult education, both formal and informal. "Lifelong Learning" programs, specifically designed for older students, are springing up in colleges and universities everywhere. Many programs are low-cost or free.

Consider retirement. You will have more time than ever before to pursue your own interests. You have an active mind and boundless curiosity. You have a foundation of knowledge gained throughout your career and family years to build upon. You're looking for fulfillment, for mental engagement. It all adds up to a renewed pursuit of knowledge. Even if you've never dreamed of going back to school, you might pick up a lecture now and then or find yourself tracking down an interesting tidbit on the web.

And remember: the best way to learn something is to teach it.

❑ Read for fun every day.

❑ Keep up with world events so I know what's going on.

❑ Read the classics I was supposed to read back in school and find out why they're great.

❑ Re-read the classics I *did* read in school and understand why they're classics—without worrying about a grade or writing a report.

❑ Pick up a catalog and see what's happening at the local community college or university.

❑ _____
_____

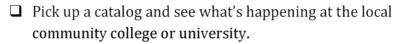

IN THEIR WORDS

Retirees tell it like it is

"My entire college education was technical—math, science, engineering. In retirement I want to learn more about the humanities—history, languages, and psychology."
--Retiring mechanical engineer

"I take several classes a year. Right now I'm completing a series of classes on comparative religion, learning about Buddhism, Islam, and Hinduism."
--Retired homemaker

❑ Learn about Osher Lifelong Learning classes for over-50s. *www.osherfoundation.org/index.php?olli*

❑ Join the faculty of my local Osher program and teach what I've spent a lifetime learning.

- ❑ *"We either live lives of inertia, or lives of expansion. The difference is intention."* —Michael Bogar

- ❑ Take an adult education course on basic auto maintenance.

- ❑ Join a book group.

- ❑ Start a book group.

- ❑ Read a "for idiots" or "for dummies" book on whatever I want to learn next (even though I'm no dummy).

- ❑ "Surf" through the encyclopedias that have been gathering dust on my bookshelf.

- ❑ Become a bona fide expert on any topic I want to pursue.

- ❑ Learn about "Access" programs for older adults at many colleges, opening the door to auditing almost any college course for peanuts.

- ❑ _____
   _____

- ❑ Sign up for a "Road Scholar" (formerly Elderhostel) program combining travel, socializing, and education, all at a manageable cost. *www.roadscholar.org*

- ❑ Be open to everything the grandkids can teach me.

- ❑ Study feng shui and bring harmony to my space.

- ❑ *"It doesn't matter what age you are. Almost everybody's at that same place, inventing or reinventing the next phase of their lives."* —Bill Burnett, Executive Director, Design Program, Stanford University

- ❑ Take an online e-learning course on anything that strikes my fancy.

- ❏ Mark on my calendar the "free" days at all my local museums.
- ❏ Take a senior driving class and count my savings on car insurance. (Check availability with AAA or AARP.)
- ❏ Vow to make every experience an opportunity to learn.
- ❏ Enroll in a college degree program and earn the degree I've always wanted.
- ❏ Learn the Dewey Decimal System and explore every part of it at the library.
- ❏ _____
_____
- ❏ Improve my computer skills.
- ❏ Tune in for everyday educational TV for everything from the basics to college-level courses.
- ❏ Learn the latest lingo from the kids, grandkids, or any young people I run into.
- ❏ See what free lectures are coming up at the library or college.
- ❏ Attend an author event at the book store.
- ❏ Listen to instructional CDs, either checked out of the library or purchased.
- ❏ Don't overlook instructional videos on DVD or online.
- ❏ _____
_____
- ❏ Access the most powerful information tool ever invented: the internet.

- [ ] Attend a political rally.

- [ ] Sign up for a lecture series.

- [ ] Attend so many online classes I can earn a degree.

- [ ] Take "shop" classes to improve my skills for car maintenance and home maintenance.

- [ ] Make education expenses tax-free by using a "Section 529" account, a Coverdell Education Savings Account, or other savings plans. Investigate at *www.savingforcollege.com.*

NOTES

CHAPTER TWELVE

RETIREMENT ACTIVITIES:
CREATE IT

Look at retirees around you. You'll find them experiencing a creativity explosion. With extra time on your hands, and with a need for fulfilling activities, you might find yourself getting more creative than ever, whether it's rearranging your space or taking up oil painting. Your creativity may have lain dormant for years, perhaps long forgotten, but all it needs is a spark. As you plan your retirement life, why not consider these many ways to express yourself?

❑ Exhibit my photographs in a show.

❑ Really get into woodworking.

❑ Throw myself into a pottery class.

❑ Write the great American novel, just for fun.

❑ Write the great American novel, and sell it.

❑ Publish a book to share the professional expertise I gained throughout my career.

❑ _____

_____

❑ Sell my watercolor paintings or oils in a gallery.

❑ *"Every person is, in part, 'his own project' and makes himself." —Abraham Maslow*

- ❑ Act up in local community theater.
- ❑ Try my hand at sculpting.
- ❑ Make my auto restoration project a work of art.
- ❑ Make a meal a work of art in my "studio"—the kitchen.
- ❑ _____
  _____

IN THEIR WORDS

Retirees tell it like it is

"I made a hobby horse for my grandson in the woodshop. Then I made some more for the neighborhood kids. Then it hit me. Now I make hobby horses and other woodcrafts in the winter, load them into the RV, and spend the summer travelling from craft fair to craft fair. Sales support the 'hobby horse hobby' and the travel."
--Retired neighbor

- ❑ Let my green thumb go wild, making my garden a show-stopper all year long.
- ❑ Dress myself with style and taste.
- ❑ Create an elegant "seasons" meal for a few friends, four times a year.
- ❑ Take that piano class I've always meant to take.

❏ *"People move in the direction of the highest vision they have of their future."* —Edward Jacobson

❏ Record my own music and learn how to make a CD to share.

❏ _____

_____

❏ Turn my favorite family photos into a bound book.

IN THEIR WORDS

Retirees tell it like it is

"Two years ago I was a labor negotiator. Now I sculpt in bronze."
--Retired business manager

❏ Make an online slide show of my favorite vacation photos to share with friends and family.

❏ Get into video recording and editing.

❏ Convert myself from a packrat to an artist by displaying my collection(s) creatively.

❏ Sign up for a digital photography class.

❏ Design marketing materials for a friend—or for my own business.

❏ _____

_____

- ❑ *"Perhaps my best years are gone…but I wouldn't want them back, not without the fire in me now." —Samuel Beckett*

- ❑ Set up a family website.

- ❑ Make my own birthday cards for every family birthday for a year.

- ❑ Get into photo-gifting with mugs, hats, or t-shirts with favorite photos.

- ❑ Create a small line of greeting cards and sell them in local shops.

- ❑ Perform my music at a local retirement home or senior center.

- ❑ _____
  _____

- ❑ Refurbish a classic travel trailer.

- ❑ Say "I love you" with a custom-made music mix featuring personal messages for a loved one.

- ❑ Move my craft to a new level of craftsmanship with the extra time I'll have.

- ❑ Let others make the art. I'll take an art-, music-, or theater-appreciation class to deepen my understanding and enjoyment.

- ❑ Build and install a series of colorful birdhouses to beautify the neighborhood.

- ❑ *"You have to reinvent yourself every day, and that means being a pioneer." —Frederic de Narp, President and CEO of Cartier*

- ❑ Become a master model-maker or diorama designer for the local museum.

- ❑ _____
  _____

- ❑ Polish my speaking skills at Toastmasters meetings, and take my talk on the road.

- ❑ Undertake creative framing of my cherished family portraits.

- ❑ Update my personal presentation portfolio.

- ❑ Complete my breakout script.

- ❑ Keep a daily blog.

- ❑ Experience writing or drawing with my non-dominant hand.

- ❑ Exercise my eye for interior design to make my living space a work of art.

- ❑ Start an audio blog—like having my own private radio station right at home.

- ❑ Publish an e-book on how to publish e-books.

- ❑ Build a bat-house for the backyard to attract these fascinating creatures. Find free plans at several sites, including *www.batconservation.org/drupal/free_plans.*

NOTES

CHAPTER THIRTEEN

RETIREMENT ACTIVITIES
GIVE IT
VOLUNTEERING AND CHARITY

Retirement offers a tremendous opportunity for volunteering or charity work. Some people are motivated by a sense that they've been "given much" from society, and look forward to giving back. Others are seeking a sense of fulfillment, or an outlet for their professional skills, or simply a structured part of their week to look forward to.

Volunteering can be anything from shelf-stocking at the food bank to highly professional work like directing the non-profit organization that sponsors the food banks in your city.

Numerous studies have found tremendous health benefits from volunteering, particularly for men. A famous 1988 University of Michigan study tracked 2700 people for 10 years. Men who did not volunteer were 2-1/2 times more likely to die during the study than men who volunteered at least once a week.

The trick is finding the volunteer job that really suits you. Here are some ideas:

❑ Assess the skills I've learned over a lifetime, think about what my community needs, and find the perfect volunteer job to combine them.

❑ Test drive a new volunteer job every year.

❑ Use my business skills to mentor others starting new businesses. See *www.score.org.*

- ❏ Check out volunteer opportunities in my local schools.

- ❏ It's all about leading tours in a museum, baby.

- ❏ Consider what the world is crying out for, and what my soul is crying out to do, and put them together.

- ❏ _____
_____

- ❏ Consider the many ways I can contribute at my place of worship.

- ❏ Find a volunteer job that satisfies my wish to "give back" for all I've been given.

- ❏ Peruse local volunteer listings for the ideal volunteer job. See *www.volunteermatch.org* and input my zip code.

- ❏ Check out everything Senior Corps is doing. See *www.seniorcorps.org.*

- ❏ Remember that the ideal volunteer job isn't just about what I can give the job, but what the job gives me.

- ❏ Serve as a role model, mentor, and friend through the Foster Grandparents program. See *www.seniorcorps.gov/about/ programs/fg.asp.*

- ❏ _____
_____

- ❏ Give the gift of companionship and help a frail senior stay independent in the Senior Companions program. See *www.seniorcorps.gov/about/programs/sc.asp.*

- ❏ Learn about volunteering and peruse volunteer jobs ideal for retirees through AARP. See *www.aarp.org/giving-back/volunteering/.*

❑ Combine my love for RVing with giving back, by serving as a Camp Host.

IN THEIR WORDS
Retirees tell it like it is

"When I first retired on disability, I literally drove my wife out of the house by turning on TV soap operas at each end of the house and walking between the TVs for exercise. I needed a life. I went out and got one: a volunteer job with the Red Cross."
--Retired high school principal

"I really wanted to fill my time by volunteering in leadership roles with non-profits. Before long I was going to so many board meetings and functions that I was TOO busy. I had to start saying no."
--Retired HR manager

❑ Check out RSVP (Retired Seniors Volunteer Program), America's largest senior volunteer network. Start at *www.seniorcorps.gov/about/programs/rsvp.asp*.

❑ _____
  _____

❑ Study how to volunteer. See *www.wikihow.com/Volunteer.*

- ❑ Read about volunteer work and paid work at Senior Living. *http://seniorliving.about.com/od/workandcareers/Retirement_Jobs_and_Volunteering_for_Baby_Boomers_and_Seniors.htm.*

- ❑ Guide the way by being a volunteer lighthouse keeper. See *www.uslhs.org/resources_be_a_keeper.php.*

- ❑ Become the children's story reader at the library.

- ❑ Be a volunteer driver to help older people get to medical appointments.

- ❑ *"We act as though comfort and luxury were the chief requirements of life, when all we need to make us happy is something to be enthusiastic about." —Charles Kingsley*

- ❑ _____
  _____

- ❑ Help out at a retirement home or nursing center and count my blessings.

- ❑ Volunteer at the local fire or police department and help with emergency services.

- ❑ Find out what kind of volunteer jobs the Red Cross offers. *www.redcross.org/en/volunteer.*

- ❑ Give my travels a charitable dimension. See *http://biddingforgood.com/* or web-search "Charity Travel."

- ❑ Go all-out by sharing my skills overseas with the Peace Corps. (No upper age limit.) See *www.peacecorps.gov.*

- ❑ Volunteer to tutor children in another state. See *www.experiencecorps.org.*

- ❑ Serve overseas for 1-12 weeks through a program like Cross Cultural Solutions. See *www.crossculturalsolutions.org/ volunteering-abroad/who/50-plus.aspx.*

- ❑ _____
  _____

- ❑ Build a life with Habitat for Humanity—in my hometown or around the world. *www.habitat.org.*

- ❑ Serve as a volunteer board member for a favorite non-profit.

- ❑ Run for a local non-paid political position, like the school board.

- ❑ Combine my love for animals with my wish to serve others by learning about therapy animals. *www.deltasociety.org.*

- ❑ Be an usher at the symphony, opera, or other arts venue, and get "paid" in free performances.

- ❑ Create a family foundation to direct my charitable dollars. Start by web-searching "family foundation."

NOTES

CHAPTER FOURTEEN

Retirement Activities
Work It
Encore Careers

Have you ever thought about a paid job as part of your retirement? Maybe it's a part-time job for fun, or starting a small business, or maybe it's a full-time "encore career" doing exactly what you've been longing to do.

A job has all the benefits of volunteering—structure, social contact, goals, and health—with an added bonus: payment! The paycheck is tangible proof of the value you give others. For some, the paycheck is a necessity. For others, it's gravy, but welcome nonetheless.

Like volunteering, the key is finding the job that motivates and fulfills you. Consider these ideas:

❑ Do what I love—and get paid for it!

❑ Fly away as a professional international tour guide. See *www.itmitourtraining.com.*

❑ Rise above it all by staffing a forest fire lookout. See *www.firelookout.org.*

❑ _____
   _____

❑ Become a teacher.

❑ *"Choose a work that you love and you won't have to work another day." –Confucius*

❑ Start the small business I've always dreamed of. Consider getting guidance from the Service Corps of Retired Executives first, at *www.score.org*.

IN THEIR WORDS
Retirees tell it like it is

"The first time I retired was from the Army. The second time was from business. Now I'm retiring from teaching. Next I'm starting an apple orchard with my son."
--Retiree with multiple encore careers

"I retired from Information Technology. Now I work two days a week at a hardware store. I love it--it's basically a bunch of us old farts hanging around and talking hardware."
--Retired I.T. engineer

"My wife and I got into seasonal tax preparation after I retired. We worked in the same office together, brought in a little money, and were active and productive during the dreary months in the Puget Sound area."
--Retired nuclear engineer

- ❏ Drive a minibus for the senior center or a retirement residence.

- ❏ *"To know what has to be done, then do it, comprises the whole philosophy of a practical life"* —*Sir William Osler*

- ❏ _____
_____

IN THEIR WORDS
Retirees tell it like it is

"I got together with four other retired executives and started a high-end winery."
--Retired executive

- ❏ Realize that "work" doesn't just mean a volunteer or paid job. It can be anything constructive I do for myself, my family, and the world.

- ❏ Spend some time identifying what my ideal work would be—but this time in terms of fulfillment, not just pay.

- ❏ Make a list of all the benefits of working, beyond the paycheck and insurance, such as social contact, structure, recognition, and so on. (See Activity 4 in the "Taking Action" chapter of this book). Mark the ones most important to you. Then look for work that will supply those benefits.

- ❑ Retire from my first career, but continue to work in the same field, in a new setting.

- ❑ _____
_____

- ❑ Transfer my skills to a new, unrelated field of work.

- ❑ *"Once you make a decision, the universe conspires to make it happen." —Ralph Waldo Emerson*

IN THEIR WORDS
Retirees tell it like it is

"I volunteered with SCORE [www.score.org] for a few years, rising to a management role. Now I teach finance classes at two different colleges."
--Retired finance manager

- ❑ Hang out my shingle as a consultant.

- ❑ Plan my work hours so the "weekends" are longer than the work weeks.

- ❑ Choose to work on the weekends, avoiding the weekend crowds at recreational sites, so I can enjoy recreation with smaller crowds when I have my weekdays off.

- ❑ Explore seasonal work like retail, a resort, or summer park ranger.

- ❑ Be "on call" like a substitute teacher.

❑ *"Age is only a number, a cipher for the records. A man can't retire his experience. He must use it. Experience achieves more with less energy and time."* —Bernard Mannes Baruch

❑ _____
_____

❑ Try temping so I'm in control of my availability.

❑ Explore "phased retirement" by reducing my hours at my current work, to enjoy part-time work, part-time retirement.
Go back to school to start my new career.

❑ Learn more about working after 50 at *www.aarp.org/work.*

❑ Surf the jobs and articles at *http://seniorjobbank.com, http://seniors4hire.org,* and *www.retirementjobs.com.*

❑ Consider the career interest and assessment tests available at *www.hollandcodes.com.*

❑ *"The most powerful force on earth is the human soul on fire. Find your passion—and go for it!"* —Dorothy Billington, Ph.D., **Life is an Attitude: How to Grow Forever**

❑ _____
_____

❑ Discover my "Signature Strengths" that will focus and expand my energy, plus other assessments from Martin Seligman Ph.D., and U. Penn., at *www.authentichappiness.sas.upenn.edu/ questionnaires.aspx* (free registration required). Try the "VIA Signature Strengths Questionnaire."

- [ ] For information on thousands of jobs, peruse the Occupational Outlook Handbook at *www.bls.gov/oco.*
- [ ] Ship out with a cruise ship job.

IN THEIR WORDS
Retirees tell it like it is

"After 32 years I retired from industry. After that I served on a number of non-profit boards, then ran the state Health Care Authority, overseeing health plans for public employees. Now I'm the state director of retirement systems, appointed by the governor."
--"Retired" HR executive

- [ ] Start over and learn the ropes with an internship—paid or unpaid.
- [ ] *"As to that leisure evening of life, I must say that I do not want it. I can conceive of no contentment of which toil is not to be the immediate parent."* —Anthony Trollope
- [ ] _____

  _____

- [ ] Recognize the "three e" advantages I bring to any job I consider: expertise, experience, and emotional intelligence.
- [ ] Go back to school to become an ordained clergyperson.

❑ Return to my previous workplace, this time as a consultant.

❑ Consider that with pension or other income, I need to earn very little to exceed my pre-retirement income. I could actually do better by retiring!

NOTES

CHAPTER FIFTEEN

RETIREMENT ACTIVITIES
USE IT OR LOSE IT
MAXIMIZING HEALTH AND FITNESS

Recent studies indicate that our genes determine perhaps 25% of our health. The other 75% comes from our lifestyle—our diet, activity level, and habits like smoking.

Life expectancy keeps rising. Average life expectancy for someone in their mid-60s is the mid-80s, or more if you're healthy. For most of us, the extra years of life are not sickly, old-age years. Rather, they're healthy, mid-life years, filled with activity, learning, and deepening relationships.

Naturally, there are no guarantees of good health. Even the fittest among us grow old and pass on. But it just makes sense to do what we can to make our retirement years as healthy as possible. After all, we want to travel, play with the grandkids, pursue a new sport, and whatever else interests us and that our health allows.

❑ Finally get in shape...

❑ ...Or at least *read* about getting in shape.

❑ Walk for all my errands.

❑ *"You can't turn back the clock. But you can wind it up again." —Bonnie Prudden*

❑ Try a simple exercise for strength and balance: stand on one foot for one minute a day, for each foot.

- ❑ Prepare for my health and safety in any natural disaster. See *www.ready.gov.*
- ❑ Aim beyond wellness to wholeness.
- ❑ _____
  _____
- ❑ *"You are only old when your memories exceed your dreams." —Carl Hammerschlag, M.D., CPAE - www.healingdoc.com*
- ❑ Every year in my birth month, schedule a wellness check-up with my doctor.
- ❑ Give race-walking a try.
- ❑ Take all my prescription bottles to my doctor to be sure I'm on the right medications—and to minimize drug interactions.
- ❑ Keep up my exercise schedule by teaming up with an exercise buddy—either human or canine.
- ❑ *"Rule 1, use it or lose it. Rule 2, abuse it and you lose it. Rule 3, no pain, no gain. Rule 4, too much pain is abuse." —Charles Wischman, MD*
- ❑ _____
  _____
- ❑ Walk the neighborhood with a trash bag and trash picker tool.
- ❑ Keep my eye on the ball by attending an annual eye exam.
- ❑ *"Life is not measured by the breaths you take. But by the moments that take your breath away." —Unknown*

- ❑ Floss every day—by keeping the floss on the TV or next to my toothbrush.

- ❑ Buckle up—every time.

- ❑ Avoid dangerous addictive drugs like daytime TV.

- ❑ Join a health club, and actually use it for more exercise than simply carrying the membership card around.

- ❑ _____
_____

- ❑ Every quarter, try a new healthy activity: yoga, karate, running, rock climbing, sailing, hiking....

- ❑ Take a bite out of dental disease by keeping my regular dental checkups.

- ❑ Follow Grandma's dietary advice: eat my fruits and veggies.

- ❑ Get my portion size under control.

- ❑ *"Time is a great healer but not a very good beautician"* —*Roadside sign, I-90 in Spokane, WA*

- ❑ Look up nutrition information on 8,000 different foods and track my own diet and exercise at *www.choosemyplate.gov/SuperTracker/*.

- ❑ Since I'm leaving the rat race, lighten up on the caffeine.

- ❑ _____
_____

- ❑ Get into the swing of golf, tennis, badminton, or pickle ball.

- ❑ Try no-cost weight-lifting: lifting my own body weight at home with sit-ups, push-ups, etc.

- ❑ *"Some people try to turn back their odometers. Not me, I want people to know "why" I look this way. I've traveled a long way and some of the roads weren't paved." —Will Rogers*

- ❑ Remember that laughter is the best medicine.

- ❑ Move it!

IN THEIR WORDS

Retirees tell it like it is

"When I was working, I always said I didn't have <u>time</u> to exercise. I couldn't use that excuse in retirement, so I finally shaped up."
--Retired administrative assistant

- ❑ *"Birthdays are good for you. Statistics show that the people who have the most live the longest." —Father Larry Lorenzoni*

- ❑ Check the bibliography in the "Resources" chapter for health books like *Younger Next Year*.

- ❑ _____
  _____

- ❑ If I lose my good health, maintain my dignity.

- ❑ Devote 9 minutes and 19 seconds to viewing the video "23-1/2 Hours" by Dr. Mike Evans, describing the #1 treatment for longevity and health. *www.youtube.com/watch?v=aUaInS6HIGo*

- ❑ Join the mall-walkers when the weather discourages outdoor walking.
- ❑ Stay healthy and hydrated, no matter what level of activity I pursue.
- ❑ Step up to a 5k walk-run event...or a 10 k run...or a mini-marathon...or...?
- ❑ _____
  _____
- ❑ *"There is no cure for birth and death save to enjoy the interval." —George Santayana*
- ❑ Get my bicycle up to shape so my bike can get me up to shape.
- ❑ Paddle a kayak.
- ❑ Row row row the boat.
- ❑ Summon the courage to sign up for a sailing class.
- ❑ Go fly a kite!
- ❑ Join a bird-watching walk.
- ❑ *"You're more likely to be happy with low dollars and good health, than the other way around." —Ken Dychtwald, Ph.D., reporting on a study of retirees.*
- ❑ _____
  _____
- ❑ Boot up and climb a mountain.
- ❑ Walk to the nearest park, around the park, and back.
- ❑ Remember that the most stressful, damaging thing a person can do is...nothing.

- ❑ *"So many people spend their health gaining wealth, and then have to spend their wealth to regain their health."* — A. J. Reb Materi

- ❑ Since so much of my health is affected by my attitude, I vow to remain young at heart, no matter what.

- ❑ *"There has been much tragedy in my life; at least half of it actually happened."* —Mark Twain

- ❑ _____
  _____

- ❑ *"One does not grow old until he believes he has more to look back on than he has to look forward to."* —Maurice Chevalier

- ❑ Give yoga a free one-week try, or attend other events. Research participating studios at *www.yogamonth.org/yogamonthcard/.*

CHAPTER SIXTEEN

THE HIGHER ME

Retirees—and older people in general—are often blessed with a perspective that is elusive to others. It may be a special sense of humor, a deeper religious strength, a comfort with themselves, or simply a calm wisdom. They have discovered their deepest values and live them.

Perhaps their years of experience, combined with less stress and more time, allow a kind of inward growth there wasn't time for during the career years. Maybe it's a natural stage in the life process.

In any case, retirement is the time in life that is uniquely suited to being truly yourself, the real you, the higher you.

It would be smart to leave room in your retirement planning for this kind of inner growth. Here are some nudges in that direction:

❑ Vow to always be *"opening out a way / Whence the imprisoned splendour may escape."* (Robert Browning)

❑ Pause to appreciate a sunset.

❑ *"What kind of life and lifestyle would make you glad to get up in the morning, and go to bed at night a 'good tired'?" —Lawrence LeShan, psychologist*

❑ _____

_____

❑ Take a class to finally learn how to meditate.

- ❑ Choose happiness.

- ❑ *"Recipe for happiness: Show up, pay attention, tell the truth, and don't be attached to the outcome." —Veda Cassells-Jones*

- ❑ Remember to practice meditation at least daily.

- ❑ *"I believe that one defines oneself by reinvention." —Henry Rollins*

- ❑ Remember that he who laughs, lasts.

- ❑ *"Retirement has been a discovery of beauty for me. I never had the time before to notice the beauty of my grandkids, my wife, the tree outside my very own front door. And, the beauty of time itself." —Hartman Jule*

- ❑ _____
  _____

- ❑ Listen to my favorite classical music and see where it takes me.

- ❑ Re-connect with my religious tradition.

- ❑ Enjoy the special feel of each season as it comes around.

- ❑ *"There is a whole new kind of life ahead, full of experiences just waiting to happen. Some call it 'retirement.' I call it bliss." —Betty Sullivan*

- ❑ _____
  _____

- ❑ Read the Bible.

- ❑ Read the Quran (Koran).

- ❑ Read the Torah.

- ❑ Read _____ and _____.

- ❑ *"When you have a dream and a plan working together in the construction of a life chapter, you have a 'mission,' a circumscribed purpose that defines your use of time and space for the duration of this particular life chapter. People with a mission know where they want to go."* –Frederic M. Hudson, **Mastering the Art of Self-Renewal**

- ❑ Start a dream journal next to my bed to gain insight into my dreaming self.

- ❑ Visit a different church, synagogue, or mosque at least once a year to learn about other ways to worship.

- ❑ _____

- ❑ *"Before you speak, listen. Before you write, think. Before you spend, earn. Before you invest, investigate. Before you criticize, wait. Before you pray, forgive. Before you quit, try. Before you retire, save. Before you die, give."* —William A. Ward

- ❑ Realize that retirement is the perfect venue for enjoying the "three universal needs" of the Self-Determination Theory of social psychology: relatedness, competence, and autonomy.

- ❑ *"We are all possibilities waiting to happen."* —Brandi Winans

- ❑ _____

- ❑ Get a "parallel Bible" so a single page can show the same passage in multiple translations, and gain a deeper understanding of the meaning behind the words.

- ❑ *"Your vision will become clear only when you can look into your own heart. Who looks outside, dreams; who looks inside, awakens." —Carl Jung*
- ❑ Take a class in World Religions and finally figure out which one is "me."

IN THEIR WORDS
Retirees tell it like it is

"Everybody wanted to know 'What are you going to do? What are you going to do?' But for me it's more about how I want to *be*."
--Retired college professor

- ❑ Spend more time in the places I feel most "whole."
- ❑ _____
  _____
- ❑ *"The human being is simultaneously that which he is and that which he yearns to be." —Abraham Maslow*
- ❑ Really listen to a friend who worships differently, and ask myself, is it really so different?
- ❑ Watch the kids at the playground and see myself, years ago, and see them, years from now.
- ❑ *"It is never too late to become what you might have been." —George Eliot*

❑ Browse books like *Appreciative Moments* by Ed Jacobson, Ph.D., so I can live every day with appreciation and gratitude. (See the "Resources" chapter of this book.)

❑ _____
_____

❑ Create a personal altar in a small corner of my home.

❑ *"The tragedy in life doesn't lie in not reaching your goal. The tragedy lies in having no goal to reach." —Benjamin Mays*

❑ Take an online quiz to learn more about my spiritual beliefs, then share answers with friends and family for a lively, respectful discussion. (Web-search "religion quiz.")

❑ *"You know you're old when you've lost all your marvels" —Merry Browne*

❑ Think of someone with totally positive regard, for as long as I can.

❑ Remember the old saw that there are only three things needed for happiness: someone to love, something to do, and something to look forward to (or hope for).

❑ _____
_____

❑ Sometimes, don't just do something, sit there.

❑ *"What you are is what you have done. What you'll be is what you do now." –Buddha*

❑ Finally forgive myself so I can get on with living.

❑ Listen to hear my life calling.

- ❑ *"Life is not about finding yourself. Life is about creating yourself." –George Bernard Shaw*

- ❑ Start a retirement journal to foster a more reflective life.

- ❑ Walk in the rain, listen, and smell.

- ❑ _____
  _____

- ❑ When the glass is half-empty, see it as still half-full.

- ❑ Take time to smell the flowers.

- ❑ *"I am not always bound to win but I am bound to be true. I am not always bound to succeed but I am bound to live up to what light I have." —Abraham Lincoln*

- ❑ Next time I talk with someone, notice the color of their eyes.

- ❑ *"Your time is limited, so don't waste it living someone else's life. Don't be trapped by dogma, which is living with the results of other people's thinking. Don't let the noise of others' opinions drown out your own inner voice. And most important, have the courage to follow your heart and intuition. They somehow already know what you truly want to become. Everything else is secondary." —Steve Jobs, 2005 Stanford Commencement Address*

- ❑ Show up for life and living.

- ❑ *Wisdom consists in doing the next thing you have to do, doing it with all your heart, and finding delight in doing it." –Meister Eckhardt*

- ❑ Plan my life from back to front: Think about what I want from my day, my month, even my retirement life, and then live my life to make it happen.

❑ Now more than ever, be sure my life aligns with my deepest values and life purpose. (Hint: Search Amazon.com for "purpose" or "purpose values" for many books about finding your life's purpose.)

❑

In spite of illness

in spite even of the archenemy sorrow,

one can remain alive

long past the usual date of disintegration

if one is unafraid of change,

insatiable in intellectual curiosity,

interested in big things,

and happy in small ways.

--Edith Wharton

❑

Tell me, what is it you plan to do

with your one wild and precious life?

--Mary Oliver

NOTES

CHAPTER SEVENTEEN

TAKING ACTION:
FOCUSING YOUR RETIREMENT VISION

Each of the following five activities offers a different perspective on your retirement vision. Each activity has helped thousands of pre-retirees or other trainees in recent decades. The activities, developed by leading experts in retirement planning and life planning, have been proven to raise awareness, draw out values, and identify life goals as you move toward an action plan for your retirement.

As you complete them, remember that your goal is to plan a retirement that is fun, fulfilling, and significant. Your answers will be incorporated in a written retirement plan in the next chapter.

Activity 1
Your Retirement Hopes and Concerns

This simple exercise, used in numerous retirement seminars internationally, will help clarify your feelings about retirement, both positive and negative, and suggest ways to plan your abundant retirement.

Simply use the columns on the next page (or a separate piece of paper) to write your Hopes and your Concerns about retirement.

Hopes	Concerns

Note: The top *concerns* mentioned by seminar participants have been fairly consistent over the years:

- Finances/Living Standard
- Health
- Boredom
- Loss of Work Relationships
- Feeling of Worthlessness
- Marital Relationship
- Loneliness
- Death and Bereavement
- Living Arrangements
- Legal Papers Not Updated

Is your list similar? Different?

This is a powerful exercise because when we're asked, "What will you do in retirement," we often mention a few top-of-mind "hopes." They might not be very well-thought-out, e.g. "Oh, I'll be on the golf course," "Taking it easy," "Fishing," or a similar remark.

We rarely talk about our "concerns." It's comforting to know that most pre-retirees share the same short list of concerns about the big change coming up.

Sometimes your "concerns" can block progress on planning for your "hopes." One goal of your retirement planning should be to address your concerns in a positive way. That will release energy to pursue your hopes.

For example, if money is a concern, how can you generate more money for your plan, and/or reduce expenses to fit a realistic projection of your retirement finances? Once that concern is addressed, you can more easily pursue your hopes to build a fun, fulfilling retirement.

Author unknown. Used by Eugene Lieberg at Boeing as early as 1976.

Activity 2
Three Questions
by George Kinder CFP® RLP®

George Kinder is the Founder of the Kinder Institute of Life Planning, and is considered the father of the Life Planning movement. He is the author of numerous books, audio recordings, and video programs. See his website at ***www.kinderinstitute.com*** *for more information about his trainings and writings.*

The start point of creating a life plan is truthfully answering three simple, yet profound, questions:

• **Question 1: Imagine you have all the money you need, now and in the future...how would you live your life?**

• **Question 2: You just found out that you only have 5 to 10 years left to live...will you change your life and how will you live it?**

• **Question 3: You just found out you only have 24 hours left to live...what regrets do you have, who did you not get to be?**

The answers to these questions reveal what people really want out of life, but may be failing to accomplish, due to a variety of "money excuses." ...the heart's core values that are revealed provide the building blocks of a meaningful life plan.

This material was developed by George Kinder and the Kinder Institute of Life Planning. It is used by financial planning professionals who hold the Registered Life Planner® (RLP®) designation. Used here by permission of George Kinder © 2006.

Activity 3
Your Retirement Business Card
By Rein Selles

Rein Selles is a Professional Retirement Planner specializing in the area of Lifestyle and Income Planning. As a teacher, Rein has taught in the faculty of Human Ecology (University of Alberta, Edmonton). In his capacity as a Pre-Retirement Educator, he has had the privilege of helping over fifty-six thousand Canadians across Canada plan their retirements through his company, Retirement/Life Challenge Ltd. He was awarded Honorary Life Membership in the Retirement Planners Association of Canada and recognized as a Distinguished Alumnus of the University of Waterloo for his contributions to the field. See his website at **www.retirementchallenge.com**, *and his book, cited below and in the "Resources" chapter.*

If someone asked you, *"What are you going to do when you retire?"* what would your answer be? Does your reply show choices that would create a meaningful and productive retirement? The following exercise is intended to get you thinking, at a personal level, about how a retirement plan is created. In the space below, you'll see a box equal to the size of a business card. On the card (or the back of an actual business card), write the following:

- **Your name** (centered—because the plan is about you, not someone else).
- **One thing you would like to do "retired"** (write this below your name). Why one? Because you can't do everything at once. You have to begin with one.

- **Where you hope to do this** (write this in the upper left hand corner). If you wrote "Travel," indicate in the top left hand corner which destination you are going to <u>first</u>.

I was teaching the retirement card exercise in Whitehorse, Yukon Territory, when an individual at the back of the room spoke up and said, *"I have one of those (cards)!"* I invited him to the front and he pulled a card out of his wallet that looked something like this:

Henry (Retired)
Toy Doctor
Repair and Refurbishing
of Well-Loved Toys

Toys donated to the
Children's Cancer Unit

"This is a wonderful retirement card!" I said as I looked at his name tag. *"But I'm confused. Your name tag says 'Tom' but the card says 'Henry.'"*

Tom replied, *"Oh, some old guy gave this to me once and I liked it so much, I kept it!"*

I wondered then, *"How many people are walking around with someone else's plans for retirement in their minds or pockets?"*

Used with permission from 10 Things I Wish Someone Had Told Me About Retirement by Rein Selles, Jim Yih and Patricia French. Published by Retirement/Life Challenge Ltd., 9 Elliot Place, St. Albert, Alberta, Canada 2nd Edition (2011).

Activity 4
"Life Benefits" From Work
By Helen Dennis

Helen Dennis is a nationally recognized expert on the issues of aging, employment and retirement. With over 20 years of academic experience at USC's Andrus Gerontology Center, she was a delegate to the White House Conference on Aging, writes a column on aging for the Daily Breeze, and has had extensive experience with the media, including Prime Time and the Wall Street Journal. She co-authored Project Renewment: The First Retirement Model for Career Women. *See* ***www.ProjectRenewment.com*** *and the "Resources" chapter of this book for more on her book.*

In the blank space below, jot down the "life benefits" you get (or used to get) by going to work. These are benefits aside from your paycheck and your employee benefits. For example, by going to work you get to socialize and get to know a wide variety of people. Give yourself five minutes to write down all the "benefits" you can think of.

Life Benefits from Work

Now look over your list. The good news is that by going to work, you have (or had) an automatic, built-in source for all these benefits. The bad news is that when you retire, you cut yourself off from all of these benefits.

Some of the benefits you listed are "nice-to-haves." Others are necessities if you want to live a full life. If you listed benefits like *goals, identity, achievement, social contact, learning,* and *appreciation,* a life lacking them would be an empty life indeed. Go back to your list and add any additional life benefits you think of, and then mark those items you really wouldn't want to live without.

Your goal in planning your retirement life is to design a life that feeds you all the life benefits you get from work. Be sure to build them into your life plan!

Used with permission from Helen Dennis,
www.HelenMDennis.com.

Activity 5
Fantasy Day in Retirement
By Karen Kent, MSG

Karen Kent is a gerontologist and licensed mental health therapist based in Seattle. In addition to managing a county-wide geriatric mental health crisis program, Karen leads dynamic retirement lifestyle planning seminars for employers and other groups.

This exercise will help you visualize your retirement in a simple, clear way. Imagine yourself one year into retirement (or, if already retired, one year from today) as you answer the following questions.

If you have a partner, it's valuable for each of you to answer the questions separately, and then compare your Fantasy Days. You'll have to accommodate *both* your visions as you plan for retirement.

Try to build into your Fantasy Day some of your retirement hopes and your answers to the "Three Questions" and "Life Benefits From Work" activities above.

When did you get up?

Where are you living?

How is the weather?

What geographic area?

Is it in the country, town, or city?

What kind of living arrangement? House, condo, mobile home?

If you have kids, how old are they?

Do they need assistance of any kind from you?

Are your parents still living?

How much help do they need from you?

What about you? Who are you living with?

How have you spent your morning?

What will you have for lunch?

Today, what things will you do for yourself for your own enjoyment or satisfaction?

What will you do this afternoon? This evening?

Do you have enough money to enjoy the things you want to do?

What do you do for others?

Who do you spend time with?

How is your health and your family's health?

In your reflections today, what things in your life did you think about that were of special importance to you?

What are you looking forward to—what goals do you have for the future?

Used with permission from Karen Kent, MSG.

CHAPTER EIGHTEEN

ABC PLANNING YOUR ABUNDANT RETIREMENT

It's time to pull together everything you've done with this book and actually design your abundant retirement life. Doing so is as easy as A, B, C:

A. Create your Retirement Wish List from the items you've checked or jotted in this book.
B. Assign a time frame to each item in the Wish List.
C. Create Your Retirement Plan by re-ordering your Wish List in chronological order.

A: Retirement Wish List

Start by creating your "Retirement Wish List." Sift back through every page in each chapter, and pull out your favorites, the very juiciest items you marked, and your favorite responses in Chapter 17's Activities. You might put a star, an asterisk, or a second checkmark beside those items that really excite you, that move you, or that you just can't live without.

Continue until you have 1-5 "must haves" from each relevant chapter, items you would love to build into your retirement life. Then jot them here, in your own words. Or start a three-ring binder, scrapbook, index card stack, or computer file to allow lots of room for organizing and re-organizing.

No, you don't have to have items from *every* chapter, for example if you don't plan to work for pay. But ideally, you'll have at least one idea from each chapter.

Go for it!

Re-Defining Retirement

1. _____

2. _____

3. _____

4. _____

5. _____

Goodbye Work, Hello Retirement!

1. _____

2. _____

3. _____

4. _____

5. _____

Location, Location, Location: Housing Choices

1. _____

2. _____

3. _____

4. _____

5. _____

Right On The Money: Dollars and Sense

1. _____

2. _____

3. _____

4. _____

5. _____

Estate Planning and My Greater Legacy

1. _____

2. _____

3. _____

4. _____

5. _____

Relationships: My Spouse/Partner

1. _____

2. _____

3. _____

4. _____

5. _____

Relationships: Kinship
Family, Kids, And Grand-Kids

1. _____

2. _____

3. _____

4. _____

5. _____

Relationships: My Social Circle

1. _____

2. _____

3. _____

4. _____

5. _____

Retirement Activities: Try It!
New Things to Try in Retirement

1. _____

2. _____

3. _____

4. _____

5. _____

Retirement Activities: Tour It
Retirement Travel

1. _____

2. _____

3. _____

4. _____

5. _____

Retirement Activities: Learn It
Lifelong Education

1. _____

2. _____

3. _____

4. _____

5. _____

Retirement Activities: Create It

1. _____

2. _____

3. _____

4. _____

5. _____

Retirement Activities: Give It
Volunteering and Charity

1. _____

2. _____

3. _____

4. _____

5. _____

Retirement Activities: Work It
Encore Careers

1. _____

2. _____

3. _____

4. _____

5. _____

Retirement Activities: Move It
Maximizing Health and Fitness

1. _____

2. _____

3. _____

4. _____

5. _____

The Higher Me

1. _____

2. _____

3. _____

4. _____

5. _____

Retirement Hopes and Concerns
Concerns to address or hopes to realize

1. _____

2. _____

3. _____

4. _____

5. _____

Three Questions
What's important to me

1. _____

2. _____

3. _____

4. _____

5. _____

Retirement Business Card
My retirement self, in brief

1. _____

2. _____

3. _____

4. _____

5. _____

"Life Benefits" From Work
Benefits to build into retirement life

1. _____

2. _____

3. _____

4. _____

5. _____

Fantasy Day in Retirement
Visualizing retirement living

1. _____

2. _____

3. _____

4. _____

5. _____

B: Retirement Planning Time Frames

Now review the items you listed in your Retirement Wish List (above). For each item, assign a time frame to explore that item or build it into your life. This isn't necessarily a "due date," but just the time you see yourself realizing that item. You can use the following suggested time frames and codes, or make your own:

A. Immediate—within the next 6 months
B. 6 months to 1 year from now
C. 1-3 years from now
D. Over 3 years from now

Write the time frame code right on your Retirement Wish List in the margin before each Wish List item.

C: Your Retirement Plan

Almost done! Finally, re-arrange all your Wish List items into their proper time frames in the spaces below (or your own separate pages or computer file). Just write all your "A" items into the "Immediate—within the next 6 months" space, and so on. It's OK to move items around if one time frame gets too full or too empty—you can't do it all in the next 6 months! Add extra pages as necessary to hold all your retirement thoughts, and add target dates for completion if you wish.

My Retirement Plan

A. Immediate — within the next 6 months

Today's Date: _____

1. _____

2. _____

3. _____

4. _____

5. _____

6. _____

7. _____

8. _____

9. _____

10. _____

11. _____

12. _____

13. _____

14. _____

15. _____

My Retirement Plan
B. 6 Months to 1 Year From Now
Today's Date: _____

1. _____

2. _____

3. _____

4. _____

5. _____

6. _____

7. _____

8. _____

9. _____

10. _____

11. _____

12. _____

13. _____

14. _____

15. _____

My Retirement Plan
C. 1-3 Years From Now
Today's Date: _____

1. _____

2. _____

3. _____

4. _____

5. _____

6. _____

7. _____

8. _____

9. _____

10. _____

11. _____

12. _____

13. _____

14. _____

15. _____

My Retirement Plan
D. Over 3 Years From Now
Today's Date: _____

1. _____

2. _____

3. _____

4. _____

5. _____

6. _____

7. _____

8. _____

9. _____

10. _____

11. _____

12. _____

13. _____

14. _____

15. _____

Congratulations!

You now have something 99% of your friends don't have: a written Retirement Plan.

Now that you've created your Retirement Plan, always keep it in mind. Photocopy it, carry it with you, photograph it into your phone, type it up on your computer, post it where you can see it frequently. Share it with your partner, and with friends when they ask "What are you going to do in retirement?" (You'll amaze them with your thoroughness!) It's yours, it's you. Look it over and dream about it often.

As an enhancement, get artistic! Add pictures of your favorite activities. Draw yourself enjoying retirement, or collect pictures that represent what you want from life. Create a "vision board"—a collage of pictures and words that move you, cut from magazines and pasted up (physically or electronically)—and hang it where you'll see it every day. (Search "vision board" on Youtube.com.)

By the way, your Plan isn't carved in stone. It can be endlessly refined and "Photoshopped" to your liking as your retirement vision evolves.

And now...*make it happen. Your abundant retirement is waiting for you.*

Retirement Planning Resources
Bibliography and Websites

Note: editorial comments reflect the unusual opinions of Andy Landis only. Always look for the most recent book edition.

GENERAL RETIREMENT

What Color Is Your Parachute? For Retirement, John Nelson and Richard Bolles. A comprehensive book covering all aspects of retirement planning, with an emphasis on lifestyle planning.

Comfort Zones: Planning a Fulfilling Retirement, Marion Haynes. A classic of general retirement planning manuals, with plenty of worksheets.

Looking Forward: An Optimist's Guide To Retirement, Ellen Freudenheim. A zillion ideas to consider for fun and fulfillment in retirement.

Project Renewment: The First Retirement Model For Career Women, Bernice Bratter & Helen Dennis. Two retirement experts address pre-boomer and boomer career women, for the first time in history facing retirement in large numbers without role models. They urge you to "lose your title and find your life."

10 Things I Wish Someone Had Told Me About Retirement, Rein Selles, Jim Yih, & Patricia French. The "bible" for Canadian retirement, including both financial information and lifestyle wisdom.

www.aarp.org. All things retirement: financial information, job searching, volunteer positions and listings, health information, member benefits, insurance products, political advocacy.

www.carp.ca. The Canadian Association for Fifty-Plus. Membership benefits, political advocacy, and community.

www.investinginhealth.com. Kol Birke's intriguing website offers a downloadable spreadsheet that allows you to track your "Total Net Worth," including such measures as friendship, hobbies, health/exercise, family, and more, in addition to the traditional financial measures.

www.retireusa.net. A "retirement resources directory" with general information about various retirement locations, organized by state. The best part: a vast collection of blogs about retirement by experts.

Personal coaches to support you in retirement life planning:

- International Coach Federation referral service: *http://coachfederation.org/clients/crs/*
- Retirement Options retirement coaches: *www.retirementoptions.com/FindACoach.asp*

TRANSITION

Transitions: Making Sense Of Life's Changes, William Bridges. The classic text on managing any and all of life's transitions, including retirement. Easy read.

HOUSING & LOCATION

Retirement Places Rated: What You Need to Know to Plan the Retirement You Deserve, David Savageau. Popular resource for relocaters. A bit dated now, but rich with information.

Housing Safety Checklist by North Carolina State University Cooperative Extension: *http://www.ces.ncsu.edu/depts/fcs/pdfs/FCS-461.pdf*

Pocket Neighborhoods: Creating Small-Scale Community in a Large-Scale World, Ross Chapin. An architect describes the concept of "smaller, smarter, community-oriented living environments."

Full-time RVing: *www.rv-dreams.com* and *www.fulltimervliving.net*

Tiny houses: *www.designboom.com/contemporary/tiny_houses.html* and *www.smallhousestyle.com*

International living: *http://internationalliving.com*

FINANCIAL

Social Security, The Inside Story, Andy Landis. The classic on Social Security and Medicare. (Shameless self-promotion? Yes.) Be sure to get the latest edition.

Money for Life and *Recession-Proof Your Retirement,* both by Steve Vernon. A former actuary gives valuable, unbiased advice. Also see Steve's website, *www.restoflife.com,* for helpful articles and links.

The Little Book of Common Sense Investing: The Only Way to Guarantee Your Fair Share of Stock Market Returns, John C. Bogle. The guru of index investing gives an accessible, common-sense overview of his simple investing philosophy.

Everything You Know About Money Is Wrong: Overcoming The Financial Myths Keeping You From The Life You Want, Karen Ramsey. The subtitle says it all. This book sets you free from misconceptions, e.g. paying for a child's college is more important than retirement savings.

Live It Up Without Outliving Your Money: 10 Steps To A Perfect Retirement Portfolio, Paul Merriman. An investment expert shares some good ideas. See also his *Financial Fitness Forever* and *www.PaulMerriman.com*.

Finish Rich series, David Bach. Pick the title(s) best for you from Bach's impressive series, all easy reads. His slogan says it all: "It's never too late to be rich!"

- *Start Late, Finish Rich: A No-Fail Plan for Achieving Financial Freedom at Any Age*
- *The Automatic Millionaire: A powerful one-step plan to live and finish rich*
- *Smart Couples Finish Rich: 9 Steps to Creating a Rich Future for You and Your Partner*
- *Smart Women Finish Rich: 9 Steps to Achieving Financial Security and Funding Your Dreams*
- *Debt Free For Life: The finish rich plan for financial freedom*
- *The Finish Rich Workbook: Creating a Personalized Plan for a Richer Future (Get out of debt, put your dreams in action and achieve financial freedom)*
- *The Automatic Millionaire Workbook: A Personalized Plan to Live and Finish Rich. . . Automatically*

The 9 Steps To Financial Freedom: Practical And Spiritual Steps So You Can Stop Worrying, Suze Orman. From the simple to the sophisticated from a well-known writer.

The Savage Number: How Much Money Do You Need To Retire, Terry Savage. All about retirement savings.

The Debt Diet: An Easy-To-Follow Plan To Shed Debt And Trim Spending, Ellie Kay. Ways to master debt.

The Wealthy Barber: The Common Sense Guide To Successful Financial Planning, David Chilton. Classic bestseller for Canadian planning.

The AARP Retirement Survival Guide, Julie Jason. A seasoned financial professional addresses retirement finances.

To find a financial planner:

- *www.fpanet.org* The Financial Planning Association, the chief professional association for financial advisors of many kinds, particularly Certified Financial Planners®.
- *www.napfa.org* Fee-only financial planners.
- *www.moneyquotient.org* Planners trained in "financial life planning."
- *www.garrettplanningnetwork.com* Pre-screened Certified Financial Planners® available by the hour.

Immediate annuities (like personalized pensions): *www.immediateannuities.com.*

Ballpark Estimator; find your retirement "number": *www.choosetosave.org/ballpark/.*

Online retirement calculators:

- *https://retirementplans.vanguard.com/VGApp/pe/pub education/calculators/RetirementIncomeCalc.jsf*
- *www.aarp.org/Retirement_Calculator*
- *www.fidelity.com/retirement/calculators*
- *www.ameriprise.com/retire/planning-for-retirement/retirement-calculators/*

A Shopper's Guide to Long-Term Care Insurance, by the National Association of Insurance Commissioners (free): *https://eapps.naic.org/forms/ipsd/Consumer_info.jsp*

Reverse Mortgages:
www.ftc.gov/bcp/edu/pubs/consumer/homes/rea13.shtm

Identity Theft: *www.fbi.gov/scams-safety/fraud/seniors* and *www.ftc.gov/idtheft*

ESTATE PLANNING

AARP Crash Course In Estate Planning: The Essential Guide To Wills, Trusts, And Your Personal Legacy, Michael T. Palermao, JD, CFP. A good intro to the topics, lingo, and concepts in estate planning. Might be good to consult before meeting with an attorney.

The Wealth of Your Life: A Step-by-Step Guide for Creating Your Ethical Will, Susan Turnbull. Workbook to create an "ethical will" to express your values, experiences, and wisdom to the next generation, rather than your material possessions and finances. See *www.YourEthicalWill.com.*

www.FamilyLoveLetter.com. This website offers a workbook for people to record all of their vital records that survivors and caretakers would need when an individual is no longer capable of giving out such information. It even includes a section for pet information.

How to Divide Your Family's Estate and Heirlooms Peacefully and Sensibly, Julie Hall. Moves from legalities like the duties of an executor to how to avoid fights over heirlooms and manage the emotional rollercoaster.

Who Gets Grandma's Yellow Pie Plate? Workbook, Marlene Stum. Suggests that most family fights are not over the money but over the family treasures that may have little economic value but enormous emotional value. A highly-recommended workbook for transferring non-titled property in a fair and peaceful way.

Five Wishes for final care:

- *www.agingwithdignity.org/five-wishes.php*
- *www.caringinfo.org*

RELATIONSHIPS

Personalized romance novels:

- *www.yournovel.com*
- *www.bookbyyou.com*

Road Scholar Family Programs: *www.roadscholar.org/programs/familyprograms.asp.*

TRAVEL

1,000 Places To See Before You Die: A Traveler's Life List, Patricia Schultz.   Must-sees organized by region.

Round the World flight tickets: *http://wikitravel.org/en/Round_the_world_flights*

Lighthouse stays: *www.uslhs.org/resources_be_a_keeper.php*

Home exchange travel: *www.homeexchange.com*

Spiritual travel:

- *www.spiritquesttours.com*
- *www.divinetravels.com*

"Gites" program for rural living in France: *http://en.gites-de-france.com/*

EDUCATION

Osher Lifelong Learning:
www.osherfoundation.org/index.php?olli

Road Scholar program (formerly Elderhostel):
www.roadscholar.org

VOLUNTEERISM

GENERAL

How to volunteer: *www.wikihow.com/Volunteer*

Volunteer and paid work article:
http://seniorliving.about.com/od/workandcareers/Retiremen t_Jobs_and_Volunteering_for_Baby_Boomers_and_Seniors.htm

Charity travel: *http://biddingforgood.com* or web-search "Charity Travel."

VOLUNTEER JOB LISTS

www.volunteermatch.org

VOLUNTEER ORGANIZATIONS

Red Cross: *www.redcross.org/en/volunteer*

Peace Corps: *www.peacecorps.gov*

Volunteer overseas for 1-12 weeks:
www.crossculturalsolutions.org/volunteering-abroad/who/50-plus.aspx

Tutor children out of state: *www.experiencecorps.org*

Mentoring start-up businesses: *www.score.org.*

Senior Corps: *www.seniorcorps.org*

- Foster Grandparents: *www.seniorcorps.gov/about/programs/fg.asp*
- Senior Companions: *www.seniorcorps.gov/about/programs/sc.asp*
- Retired Senior Volunteer Program (RSVP): *www.seniorcorps.gov/about/programs/rsvp.asp*

AARP volunteering: *www.aarp.org/giving-back/volunteering*

Lighthouse keepers: *www.uslhs.org/resources_be_a_keeper.php*

PAID WORK

GENERAL

UnRetirement: A Career Guide For The Retired, The Soon-To-Be Retired, The Never-Want-To-Be Retired, Catherine Dorton Fyok & Anne Marrs Dorton. A bit unconventional, basically how to keep working.

Work after 50: *www.aarp.org/work*

www.agelessinamerica.com - This site includes a comprehensive workbook to help mature workers re-career.

www.encore.org - This site contains a wealth of information about "encore careers" in the nonprofit sector. It also contains information about Mark Freedman's latest book, *Encore: Work That Matters in the Second Half of Life.*

Career interest and assessment: *www.hollandcodes.com*

Signature Strengths:
www.authentichappiness.sas.upenn.edu/questionnaires.aspx
(free registration required). Click on "VIA Signature
Strengths Questionnaire."

Occupational Outlook Handbook: *www.bls.gov/oco*

JOB LISTINGS

http://seniorjobbank.com/

http://seniors4hire.org/

www.retirementjobs.com/

SPECIFIC JOBS

International tour guides: *www.itmitourtraining.com*

Forest fire lookouts: *www.firelookout.org*

Starting a small business: *www.score.org*

HEALTH

Real Age: Are You As Young As You Can Be?, Michael F. Roizen, MD. How Lifestyle Choices Affect Aging. Fun quizzes and suggestions of easy changes.

Younger Next Year: A Guide To Living Like 50 Until You're 80 And Beyond, Chris Crowley & Henry S. Lodge, MD. How men can turn back their biological clocks.

Younger Next Year for Women, Chris Crowley & Henry S. Lodge, MD. Similar to above but for women.

Website for tracking diet:
www.choosemyplate.gov/SuperTracker

"23-1/2 Hours" video by Dr. Mike Evans:
www.youtube.com/watch?v=aUaInS6HIGo

THE HIGHER YOU

Appreciative Moments: Stories and Practices for Living and Working Appreciatively, Edward Jacobson, Ph.D. Small snippets of wisdom to help you appreciate every day.

SUCCESSFUL AGING

Another Country: Navigating The Emotional Terrain Of Our Elders, Mary Pipher, Ph.D. Great insights into better understanding our elders.

If I Live To Be 100: Lessons From The Centenarians, Neenah Ellis. Great interviews with those who made it to the century mark.

About the author

Andy Landis is a Certified Life Options Retirement Coach and an internationally-known author, speaker, and consultant specializing in Social Security, Medicare, and retirement lifestyle planning.

Since 1977 Andy has worked closely with pre-retirees and retirees at Social Security, AARP, a retirement residence, senior centers, Weyerhaeuser Corporation, and his own practice, Thinking Retirement.

Through Thinking Retirement, Andy conducts Social Security, Medicare, and retirement seminars for the public, employers, CPAs, financial advisors, and others.

His book, *Social Security, The Inside Story,* is hailed as the best book on the topic.

Recent projects include contributing to the web video *Investment Smarts* for PBS and AARP.

Andy lives in Seattle with Kay, keyboards, camper, computers, cars, and sometimes kids.

Follow Andy and Thinking Retirement on Facebook. Learn more at *www.andylandis.biz.*